THIS READING LOG BELONGS TO

1
2
3
4
5
6
7
8
9
10
11
12
13
14
15
16
17
18
19
20
21
22
23
24
25

26

27

28

29

30

31

32

33

34

35

36

37

38

39

40

41

42

43

44

45

46

47

48

49

50

BOOK TITLES ⟶

51
52
53
54
55
56
57
58
59
60
61
62
63
64
65
66
67
68
69
70
71
72
73
74
75

76

77

78

79

80

81

82

83

84

85

86

87

88

89

90

91

92

93

94

95

96

97

98

99

100

◯ Paperback　◯ Hardback　◯ Ebook　◯ Audiobook

Title... _____

Author... _____

◯ Fiction:　　　　　　　　　◯ Non-Fiction:

Genre. . . . . 　Subject. . . . .

| 5 | 5 | 5 | 5 | 5 | 5 | 5 | 5 | 5 | 5 | 5 | 5 | 5 | 5 | 5 | 5 | 5 | 5 | 5 | 5 | 5 | 5 | 5 | 5 | 5 | Total |
| 5 | 5 | 5 | 5 | 5 | 5 | 5 | 5 | 5 | 5 | 5 | 5 | 5 | 5 | 5 | 5 | 5 | 5 | 5 | 5 | 5 | 5 | 5 | 5 | 5 | |

Color the stars to rate this book
1 Star = Hated it　5 Stars = Loved it

What I Liked About This Book...

. . . .

. . . .

. . . .

. . . .

. . . .

. . . .

. . . .

. . . .

Date Started . . . .

Date Finished . . . .

⟵————— // —————⟶

How I Got This Book:

◯ Bought it

◯ Checked out from library

◯ Borrowed from

. . . .

◯ Gift from:

. . . .

⟵————— // —————⟶

I Was Really Surprised When...

. . . .

. . . .

. . . .

. . . .

This Book Was Easy To Read

◯ Yes　　　　◯ No

⟵————— // —————⟶

Stuff I Learned From This Book:

. . . .

. . . .

. . . .

. . . .

My Favorite Character Was...

. . . .

I Liked Them Because...

. . . .

. . . .

. . . .

Favorite Quote From The Book:

. . . .

It Was Funny/Sad/Happy When They...

. . . .

. . . .

. . . .

. . . .

. . . .

. . . .

. . . .

2

Color the stars to rate this book
1 Star = Hated it   5 Stars = Loved it

Date Started . . . .

Date Finished . . . .

←—————— // ——————→

How I Got This Book:

◌ Bought it

◌ Checked out from library

◌ Borrowed from

. . . .

◌ Gift from:

. . . .

←—————— // ——————→

This Book Was Easy To Read

◌ Yes   ◌ No

←—————— // ——————→

Stuff I Learned From This Book:

. . . .

. . . .

. . . .

. . . .

. . . .

. . . .

Favorite Quote From The Book:

. . . .

. . . .

. . . .

. . . .

. . . .

◌ Paperback   ◌ Hardback   ◌ Ebook   ◌ Audiobook

Title... _____ ✎

Author... _____ ✎

◌ Fiction: ◌ Non-Fiction:
   Genre. . . . .   Subject. . . . .

S	S	S	S	S	S	S	S	S	S	S	S	S	S	S	S	S	S	S	S	S	S	S	S	S	Total
S	S	S	S	S	S	S	S	S	S	S	S	S	S	S	S	S	S	S	S	S	S	S	S	S	

What I Liked About This Book...

. . . .

. . . .

. . . .

. . . .

. . . .

. . . .

I Was Really Surprised When...

. . . .

. . . .

. . . .

My Favorite Character Was...

I Liked Them Because...

. . . .

. . . .

It Was Funny/Sad/Happy When They...

. . . .

. . . .

. . . .

. . . .

○ Paperback ○ Hardback ○ Ebook ○ Audiobook

Title...

Author...

○ Fiction:
Genre. . . . .

○ Non-Fiction:
Subject. . . . .

| S | S | S | S | S | S | S | S | S | S | S | S | S | S | S | S | S | S | S | S | S | S | S | Total |
| S | S | S | S | S | S | S | S | S | S | S | S | S | S | S | S | S | S | S | S | S | S | S | |

3

Color the stars to rate this book
1 Star = Hated it   5 Stars = Loved it

Date Started . . . .

Date Finished . . . .

←——————— // ———————→

How I Got This Book:

○ Bought it

○ Checked out from library

○ Borrowed from

. . . .

○ Gift from:

. . . .

←——————— // ———————→

This Book Was Easy To Read

○ Yes   ○ No

←——————— // ———————→

What I Liked About This Book...

. . . .
. . . .
. . . .
. . . .
. . . .
. . . .
. . . .

Stuff I Learned From This Book:

. . . .

I Was Really Surprised When...

. . . .
. . . .
. . . .
. . . .

. . . .
. . . .

My Favorite Character Was...

. . . .

. . . .

I Liked Them Because...

. . . .
. . . .

Favorite Quote From The Book:

. . . .

It Was Funny/Sad/Happy When They...

. . . .
. . . .
. . . .
. . . .

Color the stars to rate this book
1 Star = Hated it   5 Stars = Loved it

Date Started . . . .

Date Finished . . . .

←——————//——————→

How I Got This Book:

○ Bought it

○ Checked out from library

○ Borrowed from

. . . .

○ Gift from:

. . . .

←——————//——————→

This Book Was Easy To Read
○ Yes   ○ No

←——————//——————→

Stuff I Learned From This Book:

. . . .

. . . .

. . . .

. . . .

. . . .

. . . .

Favorite Quote From The Book:

. . . .

. . . .

. . . .

. . . .

. . . .

Title... _____ ✎

Author... _____ ✎

○ Fiction: ○ Non-Fiction:

Genre. . . . .   Subject. . . . .

S	S	S	S	S	S	S	S	S	S	S	S	S	S	S	S	S	S	S	S	S	S	S	S	S	Total
S	S	S	S	S	S	S	S	S	S	S	S	S	S	S	S	S	S	S	S	S	S	S	S	S	

What I Liked About This Book...

. . . .

. . . .

. . . .

. . . .

. . . .

. . . .

. . . .

I Was Really Surprised When...

. . . .

. . . .

My Favorite Character Was...

I Liked Them Because...

. . . .

. . . .

It Was Funny/Sad/Happy When They...

. . . .

. . . .

. . . .

. . . .

○ Paperback   ○ Hardback   ○ Ebook   ○ Audiobook

Title..._____

Author..._____

○ Fiction: ○ Non-Fiction:
   Genre. . . . .   Subject. . . . .

| 5 | 5 | 5 | 5 | 5 | 5 | 5 | 5 | 5 | 5 | 5 | 5 | 5 | 5 | 5 | 5 | 5 | 5 | 5 | 5 | 5 | 5 | 5 | 5 | 5 | Total |
| 5 | 5 | 5 | 5 | 5 | 5 | 5 | 5 | 5 | 5 | 5 | 5 | 5 | 5 | 5 | 5 | 5 | 5 | 5 | 5 | 5 | 5 | 5 | 5 | 5 | |

5

Color the stars to rate this book
1 Star = Hated it   5 Stars = Loved it

What I Liked About This Book...

. . . .
. . . .
. . . .
. . . .
. . . .
. . . .
. . . .

Date Started . . . .

Date Finished . . . .

←————————//————————→

How I Got This Book:

○ Bought it

○ Checked out from library

○ Borrowed from

. . . .

○ Gift from:

. . . .

←————————//————————→

I Was Really Surprised When...

. . . .
. . . .
. . . .

This Book Was Easy To Read
○ Yes   ○ No

←————————//————————→

Stuff I Learned From This Book:

. . . .

My Favorite Character Was...

. . . .

I Liked Them Because...

. . . .
. . . .

. . . .

Favorite Quote From The Book:

It Was Funny/Sad/Happy When They...

. . . .
. . . .
. . . .
. . . .

. . . .

○ Paperback   ○ Hardback   ○ Ebook   ○ Audiobook

6

Color the stars to rate this book
1 Star = Hated it   5 Stars = Loved it

Date Started . . . .

Date Finished . . . .

←——————//——————→

How I Got This Book:

○ Bought it

○ Checked out from library

○ Borrowed from

. . . .

○ Gift from:

. . . .

←——————//——————→

This Book Was Easy To Read

○ Yes   ○ No

←——————//——————→

Stuff I Learned From This Book:

. . . .
. . . .
. . . .
. . . .
. . . .
. . . .
. . . .

Favorite Quote From The Book:

. . . .
. . . .
. . . .
. . . .
. . . .
. . . .

Title . . _ _____ ✎

Author . . _ _____ ✎

○ Fiction: ○ Non-Fiction:
   Genre . . . .   Subject . . . .

S	S	S	S	S	S	S	S	S	S	S	S	S	S	S	S	S	S	S	S	S	S	S	S	S	Total
S	S	S	S	S	S	S	S	S	S	S	S	S	S	S	S	S	S	S	S	S	S	S	S	S	

What I Liked About This Book...

. . . .
. . . .
. . . .
. . . .
. . . .
. . . .

I Was Really Surprised When...

. . . .
. . . .
. . . .

My Favorite Character Was...

I Liked Them Because...

. . . .

It Was Funny/Sad/Happy When They...

. . . .
. . . .
. . . .
. . . .

○ Paperback ○ Hardback ○ Ebook ○ Audiobook

Title..._____

Author..._____

○ Fiction: ○ Non-Fiction:
  Genre...................   Subject................

| 5 | 5 | 5 | 5 | 5 | 5 | 5 | 5 | 5 | 5 | 5 | 5 | 5 | 5 | 5 | 5 | 5 | 5 | 5 | 5 | 5 | 5 | 5 | Total |
| 5 | 5 | 5 | 5 | 5 | 5 | 5 | 5 | 5 | 5 | 5 | 5 | 5 | 5 | 5 | 5 | 5 | 5 | 5 | 5 | 5 | 5 | 5 | |

Color the stars to rate this book
1 Star = Hated it   5 Stars = Loved it

Date Started ....
Date Finished ....
←————//————→
How I Got This Book:
○ Bought it
○ Checked out from library
○ Borrowed from
  ....
○ Gift from:
  ....
←————//————→
This Book Was Easy To Read
○ Yes   ○ No
←————//————→
Stuff I Learned From This Book:

What I Liked About This Book...
....
....
....
....
....
....
....
....

I Was Really Surprised When...
....
....
....
....

My Favorite Character Was...
....

I Liked Them Because...
....
....

It Was Funny/Sad/Happy When They...
....
....
....
....

Stuff I Learned From This Book:
....
....
....
....
....
....
....

Favorite Quote From The Book:
....
....
....

○ Paperback ○ Hardback ○ Ebook ○ Audiobook

8

Color the stars to rate this book
1 Star = Hated it   5 Stars = Loved it

Date Started . . . .

Date Finished . . . .

←————————//————————→

How I Got This Book:

○ Bought it

○ Checked out from library

○ Borrowed from

. . . .

○ Gift from:

←————————//————————→

This Book Was Easy To Read
○ Yes   ○ No
←————————//————————→

Stuff I Learned From This Book:

. . . .
. . . .
. . . .
. . . .
. . . .
. . . .

Favorite Quote From The Book:

. . . .
. . . .
. . . .
. . . .
. . . .

Title.._____ ✎

Author.._____ ✎

○ Fiction: ○ Non-Fiction:
   Genre. . . . .   Subject. . . . .

S	S	S	S	S	S	S	S	S	S	S	S	S	S	S	S	S	S	S	S	S	S	S	S	S	Total
S	S	S	S	S	S	S	S	S	S	S	S	S	S	S	S	S	S	S	S	S	S	S	S	S	

What I Liked About This Book...

. . . .
. . . .
. . . .
. . . .
. . . .
. . . .

I Was Really Surprised When...

. . . .
. . . .

My Favorite Character Was...

I Liked Them Because...

. . . .
. . . .

It Was Funny/Sad/Happy When They...

. . . .
. . . .
. . . .
. . . .

◯ Paperback ◯ Hardback ◯ Ebook ◯ Audiobook

Title.._____

Author.._____

◯ Fiction: ◯ Non-Fiction:
  Genre. . . . .   Subject. . . . .

5	5	5	5	5	5	5	5	5	5	5	5	5	5	5	5	5	5	5	5	5	5	5	Total
5	5	5	5	5	5	5	5	5	5	5	5	5	5	5	5	5	5	5	5	5	5	5	

9

Color the stars to rate this book
1 Star = Hated it   5 Stars = Loved it

Date Started . . . .
Date Finished . . . .
←——————//——————→
How I Got This Book:
◯ Bought it
◯ Checked out from library
◯ Borrowed from
   . . . .
◯ Gift from:
   . . . .
←——————//——————→
This Book Was Easy To Read
◯ Yes   ◯ No
←——————//——————→
Stuff I Learned From This Book:

What I Liked About This Book...

. . . .
. . . .
. . . .
. . . .
. . . .
. . . .
. . . .
. . . .

I Was Really Surprised When...

. . . .
. . . .
. . . .
. . . .

My Favorite Character Was...

. . . .

I Liked Them Because...

. . . .
. . . .

Favorite Quote From The Book:

It Was Funny/Sad/Happy When They...

. . . .
. . . .
. . . .
. . . .

10

Color the stars to rate this book
1 Star = Hated it   5 Stars = Loved it

Date Started . . . .

Date Finished . . . .

⟵————————//——————⟶

How I Got This Book:

◌ Bought it

◌ Checked out from library

◌ Borrowed from

. . . .

◌ Gift from:

. . . .

⟵————————//——————⟶

This Book Was Easy To Read
◌ Yes   ◌ No

⟵————————//——————⟶

Stuff I Learned From This Book:

. . . .

. . . .

. . . .

. . . .

. . . .

. . . .

. . . .

Favorite Quote From The Book:

. . . .

. . . .

. . . .

. . . .

. . . .

. . . .

Title... _____ ✎

Author... _____ ✎

◌ Fiction: ◌ Non-Fiction:
  Genre. . . . .   Subject. . . . .

S	S	S	S	S	S	S	S	S	S	S	S	S	S	S	S	S	S	S	S	S	S	S	S	Total
S	S	S	S	S	S	S	S	S	S	S	S	S	S	S	S	S	S	S	S	S	S	S	S	

What I Liked About This Book...

. . . .

. . . .

. . . .

. . . .

. . . .

. . . .

. . . .

I Was Really Surprised When...

. . . .

. . . .

. . . .

My Favorite Character Was...

I Liked Them Because...

. . . .

. . . .

It Was Funny/Sad/Happy When They...

. . . .

. . . .

. . . .

. . . .

○ Paperback   ○ Hardback   ○ Ebook   ○ Audiobook

Title..._____

Author..._____

○ Fiction: ○ Non-Fiction:
   Genre. . . . .   Subject. . . . .

5	5	5	5	5	5	5	5	5	5	5	5	5	5	5	5	5	5	5	5	5	5	5	5	5	Total
5	5	5	5	5	5	5	5	5	5	5	5	5	5	5	5	5	5	5	5	5	5	5	5	5	

Color the stars to rate this book
1 Star = Hated it   5 Stars = Loved it

What I Liked About This Book...

. . . .
. . . .
. . . .
. . . .
. . . .
. . . .
. . . .

Date Started . . . .
Date Finished . . . .
←————— // —————→
How I Got This Book:
○ Bought it
○ Checked out from library
○ Borrowed from
   . . . .
○ Gift from:
   . . . .
←————— // —————→

I Was Really Surprised When...

. . . .
. . . .
. . . .

This Book Was Easy To Read
○ Yes   ○ No
←————— // —————→
Stuff I Learned From This Book:

. . . .
. . . .

My Favorite Character Was...

. . . .

I Liked Them Because...

. . . .
. . . .

. . . .

. . . .

Favorite Quote From The Book:

. . . .

It Was Funny/Sad/Happy When They...

. . . .
. . . .
. . . .
. . . .

12

Color the stars to rate this book
1 Star = Hated it   5 Stars = Loved it

Date Started . . . .

Date Finished . . . .

←————————//————————→

How I Got This Book:

○ Bought it

○ Checked out from library

○ Borrowed from

. . . .

○ Gift from:

. . . .

←————————//————————→

This Book Was Easy To Read
○ Yes   ○ No

←————————//————————→

Stuff I Learned From This Book:

. . . .

. . . .

. . . .

. . . .

. . . .

. . . .

Favorite Quote From The Book:

. . . .

. . . .

. . . .

. . . .

. . . .

Title... _____ ✎

Author... _____ ✎

○ Fiction: ○ Non-Fiction:
  Genre. . . . .   Subject. . . . .

5	5	5	5	5	5	5	5	5	5	5	5	5	5	5	5	5	5	5	5	5	5	5	5	Total
5	5	5	5	5	5	5	5	5	5	5	5	5	5	5	5	5	5	5	5	5	5	5	5	

What I Liked About This Book...

. . . .

. . . .

. . . .

. . . .

. . . .

. . . .

I Was Really Surprised When...

. . . .

. . . .

My Favorite Character Was...

. . . .

I Liked Them Because...

. . . .

. . . .

It Was Funny/Sad/Happy When They...

. . . .

. . . .

. . . .

. . . .

○ Paperback ○ Hardback ○ Ebook ○ Audiobook

Title... _____

Author... _____

○ Fiction: ○ Non-Fiction:
   Genre. . . . .   Subject. . . . .

| S | S | S | S | S | S | S | S | S | S | S | S | S | S | S | S | S | S | S | S | S | S | S | S | S | S | S | Total |
| S | S | S | S | S | S | S | S | S | S | S | S | S | S | S | S | S | S | S | S | S | S | S | S | S | S | S | |

What I Liked About This Book...

. . . .
. . . .
. . . .
. . . .
. . . .
. . . .
. . . .

I Was Really Surprised When...

. . . .
. . . .
. . . .

My Favorite Character Was...

I Liked Them Because...

. . . .

It Was Funny/Sad/Happy When They...

. . . .
. . . .
. . . .
. . . .

13

Color the stars to rate this book
1 Star = Hated it   5 Stars = Loved it

Date Started . . . .

Date Finished. . . . .
←————— // —————→

How I Got This Book:

○ Bought it

○ Checked out from library

○ Borrowed from

. . . .
○ Gift from:

. . . .
←————— // —————→

This Book Was Easy To Read
○ Yes   ○ No
←————— // —————→

Stuff I Learned From This Book:

. . . .
. . . .
. . . .
. . . .

Favorite Quote From The Book:

. . . .
. . . .
. . . .
. . . .
. . . .

○ Paperback ○ Hardback ○ Ebook ○ Audiobook

14

Color the stars to rate this book
1 Star = Hated it   5 Stars = Loved it

Title..._____

Author..._____

○ Fiction:
   Genre................

○ Non-Fiction:
   Subject................

Date Started . . . .

Date Finished . . . .

5	5	5	5	5	5	5	5	5	5	5	5	5	5	5	5	5	5	5	5	5	5	5	5	5	Total
5	5	5	5	5	5	5	5	5	5	5	5	5	5	5	5	5	5	5	5	5	5	5	5	5	

←————— // —————→

How I Got This Book:

○ Bought it

○ Checked out from library

○ Borrowed from
   . . . .

○ Gift from:
   . . . .

←————— // —————→

This Book Was Easy To Read
○ Yes   ○ No

←————— // —————→

Stuff I Learned From This Book:

. . . .

. . . .

. . . .

. . . .

. . . .

. . . .

Favorite Quote From The Book:

. . . .

. . . .

. . . .

. . . .

. . . .

What I Liked About This Book...

. . . .

. . . .

. . . .

. . . .

. . . .

. . . .

. . . .

I Was Really Surprised When...

. . . .

. . . .

. . . .

My Favorite Character Was...

. . . .

I Liked Them Because...

. . . .

. . . .

It Was Funny/Sad/Happy When They...

. . . .

. . . .

. . . .

. . . .

○ Paperback ○ Hardback ○ Ebook ○ Audiobook

Title..._____ ✎

Author.._____ ✎

○ Fiction: ○ Non-Fiction:
   Genre................   Subject................

5	5	5	5	5	5	5	5	5	5	5	5	5	5	5	5	5	5	5	5	5	5	5	5	Total
5	5	5	5	5	5	5	5	5	5	5	5	5	5	5	5	5	5	5	5	5	5	5	5	

What I Liked About This Book...

....
....
....
....
....
....
....

I Was Really Surprised When...

....
....
....
....

My Favorite Character Was...

....

I Liked Them Because...

....
....
....

It Was Funny/Sad/Happy When They...

....
....
....
....

15

Color the stars to rate this book
1 Star = Hated it   5 Stars = Loved it

Date Started...............

Date Finished...............
←————//————→
How I Got This Book:
○ Bought it
○ Checked out from library
○ Borrowed from
   ....
○ Gift from:
   ....
←————//————→
This Book Was Easy To Read
○ Yes   ○ No
←————//————→
Stuff I Learned From This Book:
....
....
....
....
....

Favorite Quote From The Book:
....
....

○ Paperback ○ Hardback ○ Ebook ○ Audiobook

16

Color the stars to rate this book
1 Star = Hated it   5 Stars = Loved it

Date Started . . . .

Date Finished . . . .

←————————//————————→

How I Got This Book:

○ Bought it

○ Checked out from library

○ Borrowed from

. . . .

○ Gift from:

. . . .

←————————//————————→

This Book Was Easy To Read

○ Yes   ○ No

←————————//————————→

Stuff I Learned From This Book:

. . . .

. . . .

. . . .

. . . .

. . . .

. . . .

Favorite Quote From The Book:

. . . .

. . . .

. . . .

. . . .

. . . .

. . . .

Title... _____ ✐

Author... _____ ✐

○ Fiction: ○ Non-Fiction:

Genre. . . . .   Subject. . . . .

5	5	5	5	5	5	5	5	5	5	5	5	5	5	5	5	5	5	5	5	5	5	5	5	Total
5	5	5	5	5	5	5	5	5	5	5	5	5	5	5	5	5	5	5	5	5	5	5	5	

What I Liked About This Book...

. . . .

. . . .

. . . .

. . . .

. . . .

. . . .

I Was Really Surprised When...

. . . .

. . . .

My Favorite Character Was...

I Liked Them Because...

. . . .

. . . .

It Was Funny/Sad/Happy When They...

. . . .

. . . .

. . . .

. . . .

○ Paperback ○ Hardback ○ Ebook ○ Audiobook

Title..._____

Author.._____

○ Fiction: ○ Non-Fiction:
  Genre. . . . .   Subject. . . . .

5	5	5	5	5	5	5	5	5	5	5	5	5	5	5	5	5	5	5	5	5	5	5	5	5	5	Total
5	5	5	5	5	5	5	5	5	5	5	5	5	5	5	5	5	5	5	5	5	5	5	5	5	5	

17

Color the stars to rate this book
1 Star = Hated it   5 Stars = Loved it

Date Started . . . .

Date Finished. . . . .

←————//————→

How I Got This Book:

○ Bought it

○ Checked out from library

○ Borrowed from
  . . . .

○ Gift from:
  . . . .

←————//————→

This Book Was Easy To Read
○ Yes   ○ No

←————//————→

What I Liked About This Book...

. . . .
. . . .
. . . .
. . . .
. . . .
. . . .
. . . .

I Was Really Surprised When...

Stuff I Learned From This Book:

. . . .
. . . .
. . . .
. . . .

My Favorite Character Was...

I Liked Them Because...

. . . .
. . . .

Favorite Quote From The Book:

It Was Funny/Sad/Happy When They...

. . . .
. . . .
. . . .
. . . .

18

Color the stars to rate this book
1 Star = Hated it   5 Stars = Loved it

Date Started . . . .

Date Finished . . . .

How I Got This Book:

○ Bought it

○ Checked out from library

○ Borrowed from

. . . .

○ Gift from:

. . . .

This Book Was Easy To Read
○ Yes   ○ No

Stuff I Learned From This Book:

. . . .
. . . .
. . . .
. . . .
. . . .
. . . .

Favorite Quote From The Book:

. . . .
. . . .
. . . .
. . . .
. . . .

Title . . . _____

Author . . . _____

○ Fiction: ○ Non-Fiction:
   Genre . . . .   Subject . . . .

S	S	S	S	S	S	S	S	S	S	S	S	S	S	S	S	S	S	S	S	S	S	S	S	S	Total
S	S	S	S	S	S	S	S	S	S	S	S	S	S	S	S	S	S	S	S	S	S	S	S	S	

What I Liked About This Book...

. . . .
. . . .
. . . .
. . . .
. . . .
. . . .
. . . .

I Was Really Surprised When...

. . . .
. . . .
. . . .

My Favorite Character Was...

I Liked Them Because...

. . . .

It Was Funny/Sad/Happy When They...

. . . .
. . . .
. . . .
. . . .

○ Paperback ○ Hardback ○ Ebook ○ Audiobook

Title..._____

Author..._____

○ Fiction: ○ Non-Fiction:
  Genre..............   Subject..................

5	5	5	5	5	5	5	5	5	5	5	5	5	5	5	5	5	5	5	5	5	5	5	5	5	Total
5	5	5	5	5	5	5	5	5	5	5	5	5	5	5	5	5	5	5	5	5	5	5	5	5	

What I Liked About This Book...

. . . .
. . . .
. . . .
. . . .
. . . .
. . . .
. . . .

I Was Really Surprised When...

. . . .
. . . .
. . . .
. . . .

My Favorite Character Was...

. . . .

I Liked Them Because...

. . . .
. . . .

It Was Funny/Sad/Happy When They...

. . . .
. . . .
. . . .
. . . .

19

Color the stars to rate this book
1 Star = Hated it   5 Stars = Loved it

Date Started . . . .

Date Finished . . . .

How I Got This Book:

○ Bought it

○ Checked out from library

○ Borrowed from

. . . .

○ Gift from:

. . . .

This Book Was Easy To Read
○ Yes   ○ No

Stuff I Learned From This Book:

. . . .
. . . .
. . . .
. . . .
. . . .

Favorite Quote From The Book:

. . . .
. . . .
. . . .
. . . .

○ Paperback ○ Hardback ○ Ebook ○ Audiobook

20

Color the stars to rate this book
1 Star = Hated it   5 Stars = Loved it

Date Started . . . .

Date Finished . . . .

←——————— // ———————→

How I Got This Book:

○ Bought it

○ Checked out from library

○ Borrowed from

. . . .

○ Gift from:

. . . .

←——————— // ———————→

This Book Was Easy To Read

○ Yes   ○ No

←——————— // ———————→

Stuff I Learned From This Book:

. . . .

. . . .

. . . .

. . . .

. . . .

. . . .

Favorite Quote From The Book:

. . . .

. . . .

. . . .

. . . .

. . . .

Title... _____ ✏

Author... _____ ✏

○ Fiction: ○ Non-Fiction:
   Genre. . . . .   Subject. . . . .

5	5	5	5	5	5	5	5	5	5	5	5	5	5	5	5	5	5	5	5	5	5	5	5	5	Total
5	5	5	5	5	5	5	5	5	5	5	5	5	5	5	5	5	5	5	5	5	5	5	5	5	

What I Liked About This Book...

. . . .

. . . .

. . . .

. . . .

. . . .

. . . .

I Was Really Surprised When...

. . . .

. . . .

. . . .

My Favorite Character Was...

I Liked Them Because...

. . . .

. . . .

It Was Funny/Sad/Happy When They...

. . . .

. . . .

. . . .

○ Paperback ○ Hardback ○ Ebook ○ Audiobook

Title..._____

Author..._____

○ Fiction: ○ Non-Fiction:
   Genre............   Subject...............

5	5	5	5	5	5	5	5	5	5	5	5	5	5	5	5	5	5	5	5	5	5	5	5	5	5	Total
5	5	5	5	5	5	5	5	5	5	5	5	5	5	5	5	5	5	5	5	5	5	5	5	5	5	

What I Liked About This Book...

....
....
....
....
....
....
....
....

I Was Really Surprised When...

....
....
....
....

My Favorite Character Was...

I Liked Them Because...

....
....

It Was Funny/Sad/Happy When They...

....
....
....
....

21

Color the stars to rate this book
1 Star = Hated it   5 Stars = Loved it

Date Started ....

Date Finished...............

←——————//——————→

How I Got This Book:

○ Bought it

○ Checked out from library

○ Borrowed from

....

○ Gift from:

....

←——————//——————→

This Book Was Easy To Read
○ Yes   ○ No

←——————//——————→

Stuff I Learned From This Book:

....
....
....
....
....

Favorite Quote From The Book:

....
....
....

22

Color the stars to rate this book
1 Star = Hated it   5 Stars = Loved it

Date Started . . . .

Date Finished . . . .

⟵————————//————————⟶

How I Got This Book:

◌ Bought it

◌ Checked out from library

◌ Borrowed from

. . . .

◌ Gift from:

. . . .

⟵————————//————————⟶

This Book Was Easy To Read

◌ Yes   ◌ No

⟵————————//————————⟶

Stuff I Learned From This Book:

. . . .

. . . .

. . . .

. . . .

. . . .

Favorite Quote From The Book:

. . . .

. . . .

. . . .

. . . .

. . . .

◌ Paperback   ◌ Hardback   ◌ Ebook   ◌ Audiobook

Title... _____

Author... _____

◌ Fiction: ◌ Non-Fiction:

   Genre. . . . .   Subject. . . . .

S	S	S	S	S	S	S	S	S	S	S	S	S	S	S	S	S	S	S	S	S	S	S	S	S	Total
S	S	S	S	S	S	S	S	S	S	S	S	S	S	S	S	S	S	S	S	S	S	S	S	S	

What I Liked About This Book...

. . . .

. . . .

. . . .

. . . .

. . . .

. . . .

I Was Really Surprised When...

. . . .

. . . .

. . . .

My Favorite Character Was...

I Liked Them Because...

. . . .

. . . .

It Was Funny/Sad/Happy When They...

. . . .

. . . .

. . . .

. . . .

○ Paperback   ○ Hardback   ○ Ebook   ○ Audiobook

Title..._____

Author..._____

○ Fiction: ○ Non-Fiction:
   Genre.................   Subject.................

5	5	5	5	5	5	5	5	5	5	5	5	5	5	5	5	5	5	5	5	5	5	5	5	5	Total
5	5	5	5	5	5	5	5	5	5	5	5	5	5	5	5	5	5	5	5	5	5	5	5	5	

What I Liked About This Book...

....
....
....
....
....
....
....

I Was Really Surprised When...

....
....
....
....

My Favorite Character Was...

....

I Liked Them Because...

....
....
....

It Was Funny/Sad/Happy When They...

....
....
....
....

23

Color the stars to rate this book
1 Star = Hated it   5 Stars = Loved it

Date Started ....

Date Finished...............
←————//————→
How I Got This Book:
○ Bought it
○ Checked out from library
○ Borrowed from
  ....
○ Gift from:
  ....
←————//————→
This Book Was Easy To Read
○ Yes   ○ No
←————//————→
Stuff I Learned From This Book:
....
....
....
....
....
....

Favorite Quote From The Book:
....
....
....

○ Paperback ○ Hardback ○ Ebook ○ Audiobook

24

Color the stars to rate this book
1 Star = Hated it   5 Stars = Loved it

Date Started . . . .

Date Finished . . . .

⟵————//————⟶

How I Got This Book:

○ Bought it

○ Checked out from library

○ Borrowed from

. . . .

○ Gift from:

. . . .

⟵————//————⟶

This Book Was Easy To Read

○ Yes   ○ No

⟵————//————⟶

Stuff I Learned From This Book:

. . . .

. . . .

. . . .

. . . .

. . . .

. . . .

Favorite Quote From The Book:

. . . .

. . . .

. . . .

. . . .

. . . .

. . . .

Title... _____

Author... _____

○ Fiction: ○ Non-Fiction:

Genre. . . . .   Subject. . . . .

S	S	S	S	S	S	S	S	S	S	S	S	S	S	S	S	S	S	S	S	S	S	S	S	S	Total
S	S	S	S	S	S	S	S	S	S	S	S	S	S	S	S	S	S	S	S	S	S	S	S	S	

What I Liked About This Book...

. . . .

. . . .

. . . .

. . . .

. . . .

. . . .

I Was Really Surprised When...

. . . .

. . . .

My Favorite Character Was...

. . . .

I Liked Them Because...

. . . .

. . . .

It Was Funny/Sad/Happy When They...

. . . .

. . . .

. . . .

○ Paperback   ○ Hardback   ○ Ebook   ○ Audiobook

Title... _____

Author... _____

○ Fiction: ○ Non-Fiction:
  Genre. . . . .   Subject. . . . .

S	S	S	S	S	S	S	S	S	S	S	S	S	S	S	S	S	S	S	S	S	S	S	S	S	S	S	S	S	S	Total
S	S	S	S	S	S	S	S	S	S	S	S	S	S	S	S	S	S	S	S	S	S	S	S	S	S	S	S	S	S	

What I Liked About This Book...

. . . .
. . . .
. . . .
. . . .
. . . .
. . . .
. . . .

I Was Really Surprised When...

. . . .
. . . .
. . . .
. . . .

My Favorite Character Was...

I Liked Them Because...

. . . .
. . . .

It Was Funny/Sad/Happy When They...

. . . .
. . . .
. . . .
. . . .

25

Color the stars to rate this book
1 Star = Hated it   5 Stars = Loved it

Date Started . . . .

Date Finished . . . .

How I Got This Book:

○ Bought it

○ Checked out from library

○ Borrowed from

. . . .

○ Gift from:

. . . .

This Book Was Easy To Read
○ Yes   ○ No

Stuff I Learned From This Book:

. . . .
. . . .
. . . .
. . . .
. . . .
. . . .

Favorite Quote From The Book:

. . . .
. . . .
. . . .
. . . .

26

Color the stars to rate this book
1 Star = Hated it   5 Stars = Loved it

Date Started . . . .

Date Finished . . . .

⟵—————//—————⟶

How I Got This Book:

◯ Bought it

◯ Checked out from library

◯ Borrowed from

. . . .

◯ Gift from:

. . . .

⟵—————//—————⟶

This Book Was Easy To Read

◯ Yes   ◯ No

⟵—————//—————⟶

Stuff I Learned From This Book:

. . . .

. . . .

. . . .

. . . .

. . . .

Favorite Quote From The Book:

. . . .

. . . .

. . . .

. . . .

Title... _____ ✎

Author... _____ ✎

◯ Fiction: ◯ Non-Fiction:
   Genre . . . .   Subject . . . .

S	S	S	S	S	S	S	S	S	S	S	S	S	S	S	S	S	S	S	S	S	S	S	S	S	Total
S	S	S	S	S	S	S	S	S	S	S	S	S	S	S	S	S	S	S	S	S	S	S	S	S	

What I Liked About This Book...

. . . .

. . . .

. . . .

. . . .

. . . .

. . . .

I Was Really Surprised When...

. . . .

. . . .

. . . .

My Favorite Character Was...

I Liked Them Because...

. . . .

. . . .

It Was Funny/Sad/Happy When They...

. . . .

. . . .

. . . .

. . . .

○ Paperback   ○ Hardback   ○ Ebook   ○ Audiobook

Title..._____

Author..._____

○ Fiction: ○ Non-Fiction:
   Genre...............   Subject...............

5	5	5	5	5	5	5	5	5	5	5	5	5	5	5	5	5	5	5	5	5	5	Total
5	5	5	5	5	5	5	5	5	5	5	5	5	5	5	5	5	5	5	5	5	5	

27

Color the stars to rate this book
1 Star = Hated it   5 Stars = Loved it

Date Started ....

Date Finished...............

How I Got This Book:

○ Bought it

○ Checked out from library

○ Borrowed from
....

○ Gift from:
....

This Book Was Easy To Read
○ Yes   ○ No

Stuff I Learned From This Book:
....
....
....

What I Liked About This Book...
....
....
....
....
....
....
....
....

I Was Really Surprised When...
....
....
....

My Favorite Character Was...

I Liked Them Because...
....
....

Favorite Quote From The Book:
....
....

It Was Funny/Sad/Happy When They...
....
....
....
....

◯ Paperback ◯ Hardback ◯ Ebook ◯ Audiobook

28

Color the stars to rate this book
1 Star = Hated it   5 Stars = Loved it

Date Started . . . .

Date Finished . . . .

←——————//——————→

How I Got This Book:

◯ Bought it

◯ Checked out from library

◯ Borrowed from

. . . .

◯ Gift from:

. . . .

←——————//——————→

This Book Was Easy To Read

◯ Yes   ◯ No

←——————//——————→

Stuff I Learned From This Book:

. . . .

. . . .

. . . .

. . . .

. . . .

. . . .

Favorite Quote From The Book:

. . . .

. . . .

. . . .

. . . .

. . . .

Title.._____ ✎

Author.._____ ✎

◯ Fiction: ◯ Non-Fiction:
  Genre. . . . .   Subject. . . . .

S	S	S	S	S	S	S	S	S	S	S	S	S	S	S	S	S	S	S	S	S	S	S	S	S	Total
S	S	S	S	S	S	S	S	S	S	S	S	S	S	S	S	S	S	S	S	S	S	S	S	S	

What I Liked About This Book...

. . . .

. . . .

. . . .

. . . .

. . . .

. . . .

I Was Really Surprised When...

. . . .

. . . .

My Favorite Character Was...

. . . .

I Liked Them Because...

. . . .

It Was Funny/Sad/Happy When They...

. . . .

. . . .

. . . .

○ Paperback ○ Hardback ○ Ebook ○ Audiobook

Title..._____

Author..._____

○ Fiction: ○ Non-Fiction:
  Genre. . . . .   Subject. . . . .

| 5 | 5 | 5 | 5 | 5 | 5 | 5 | 5 | 5 | 5 | 5 | 5 | 5 | 5 | 5 | 5 | 5 | 5 | 5 | 5 | 5 | 5 | 5 | 5 | Total |
| 5 | 5 | 5 | 5 | 5 | 5 | 5 | 5 | 5 | 5 | 5 | 5 | 5 | 5 | 5 | 5 | 5 | 5 | 5 | 5 | 5 | 5 | 5 | 5 | |

29

Color the stars to rate this book
1 Star = Hated it   5 Stars = Loved it

What I Liked About This Book...

. . . .
. . . .
. . . .
. . . .
. . . .
. . . .

Date Started . . . .
Date Finished. . . . .
←————————//————————→
How I Got This Book:
○ Bought it
○ Checked out from library
○ Borrowed from

. . . .
○ Gift from:

. . . .
←————————//————————→

I Was Really Surprised When...

. . . .
. . . .
. . . .
. . . .

This Book Was Easy To Read
○ Yes   ○ No
←————————//————————→
Stuff I Learned From This Book:

. . . .
. . . .
. . . .

My Favorite Character Was...

I Liked Them Because...

. . . .
. . . .

. . . .
. . . .

Favorite Quote From The Book:

It Was Funny/Sad/Happy When They...

. . . .
. . . .
. . . .
. . . .

. . . .
. . . .
. . . .

○ Paperback ○ Hardback ○ Ebook ○ Audiobook

30

Color the stars to rate this book
1 Star = Hated it   5 Stars = Loved it

Date Started . . . .

Date Finished . . . .

⟵————//————⟶

How I Got This Book:

○ Bought it

○ Checked out from library

○ Borrowed from

. . . .

○ Gift from:

. . . .

⟵————//————⟶

This Book Was Easy To Read

○ Yes   ○ No

⟵————//————⟶

Stuff I Learned From This Book:

. . . .

. . . .

. . . .

. . . .

. . . .

. . . .

Favorite Quote From The Book:

. . . .

. . . .

. . . .

. . . .

. . . .

Title... _____ ✏

Author... _____ ✏

○ Fiction: ○ Non-Fiction:

Genre. . . . .   Subject. . . . .

S	S	S	S	S	S	S	S	S	S	S	S	S	S	S	S	S	S	S	S	S	S	S	S	S	Total
S	S	S	S	S	S	S	S	S	S	S	S	S	S	S	S	S	S	S	S	S	S	S	S	S	

What I Liked About This Book...

. . . .

. . . .

. . . .

. . . .

. . . .

. . . .

I Was Really Surprised When...

. . . .

. . . .

. . . .

My Favorite Character Was...

I Liked Them Because...

. . . .

. . . .

It Was Funny/Sad/Happy When They...

. . . .

. . . .

. . . .

○ Paperback ○ Hardback ○ Ebook ○ Audiobook

Title..._____

Author..._____

○ Fiction: ○ Non-Fiction:
  Genre.....................   Subject.................

S	S	S	S	S	S	S	S	S	S	S	S	S	S	S	S	S	S	S	S	S	S	S	S	S	S	S	Total
S	S	S	S	S	S	S	S	S	S	S	S	S	S	S	S	S	S	S	S	S	S	S	S	S	S	S	

31

Color the stars to rate this book
1 Star = Hated it   5 Stars = Loved it

What I Liked About This Book...

....
....
....
....
....
....
....

Date Started ....
Date Finished...............

How I Got This Book:
○ Bought it
○ Checked out from library
○ Borrowed from
  ....
○ Gift from:
  ....

This Book Was Easy To Read
○ Yes   ○ No

I Was Really Surprised When...

....
....
....
....

Stuff I Learned From This Book:

....
....
....

My Favorite Character Was...

....

....

I Liked Them Because...

....
....

Favorite Quote From The Book:

It Was Funny/Sad/Happy When They...

....
....
....
....

....

32

Color the stars to rate this book
1 Star = Hated it   5 Stars = Loved it

Date Started . . . .

Date Finished . . . .

←———————— // ————————→

How I Got This Book:

○ Bought it

○ Checked out from library

○ Borrowed from

. . . .

○ Gift from:

. . . .

←———————— // ————————→

This Book Was Easy To Read

○ Yes   ○ No

←———————— // ————————→

Stuff I Learned From This Book:

. . . .

. . . .

. . . .

. . . .

. . . .

. . . .

Favorite Quote From The Book:

. . . .

. . . .

. . . .

. . . .

. . . .

○ Paperback   ○ Hardback   ○ Ebook   ○ Audiobook

Title... _____

Author... _____

○ Fiction: ○ Non-Fiction:
   Genre. . . . .   Subject. . . . .

S	S	S	S	S	S	S	S	S	S	S	S	S	S	S	S	S	S	S	S	S	S	S	S	S	Total
S	S	S	S	S	S	S	S	S	S	S	S	S	S	S	S	S	S	S	S	S	S	S	S	S	

What I Liked About This Book...

. . . .

. . . .

. . . .

. . . .

. . . .

. . . .

. . . .

I Was Really Surprised When...

. . . .

. . . .

My Favorite Character Was...

I Liked Them Because...

. . . .

. . . .

It Was Funny/Sad/Happy When They...

. . . .

. . . .

. . . .

. . . .

◯ Paperback ◯ Hardback ◯ Ebook ◯ Audiobook

Title..._____

Author.._____

◯ Fiction: ◯ Non-Fiction:
  Genre. . . . .   Subject. . . . .

5	5	5	5	5	5	5	5	5	5	5	5	5	5	5	5	5	5	5	5	5	5	5	5	5	Total
5	5	5	5	5	5	5	5	5	5	5	5	5	5	5	5	5	5	5	5	5	5	5	5	5	

33

Color the stars to rate this book
1 Star = Hated it   5 Stars = Loved it

What I Liked About This Book...

. . . .
. . . .
. . . .
. . . .
. . . .
. . . .
. . . .

I Was Really Surprised When...

. . . .
. . . .
. . . .

My Favorite Character Was...

I Liked Them Because...

. . . .
. . . .

It Was Funny/Sad/Happy When They...

. . . .
. . . .
. . . .
. . . .

Date Started . . . .

Date Finished . . . .
◀─────────//─────────▶

How I Got This Book:
◯ Bought it
◯ Checked out from library
◯ Borrowed from
  . . . .
◯ Gift from:
  . . . .
◀─────────//─────────▶

This Book Was Easy To Read
◯ Yes   ◯ No
◀─────────//─────────▶

Stuff I Learned From This Book:

. . . .
. . . .
. . . .
. . . .
. . . .

Favorite Quote From The Book:

. . . .
. . . .
. . . .
. . . .

34

Color the stars to rate this book
I Star = Hated it   5 Stars = Loved it

Date Started . . . .

Date Finished . . . .

How I Got This Book:

◯ Bought it

◯ Checked out from library

◯ Borrowed from

. . . .

◯ Gift from:

. . . .

This Book Was Easy To Read

◯ Yes   ◯ No

Stuff I Learned From This Book:

. . . .
. . . .
. . . .
. . . .
. . . .
. . . .
. . . .

Favorite Quote From The Book:

. . . .
. . . .
. . . .
. . . .

◯ Paperback   ◯ Hardback   ◯ Ebook   ◯ Audiobook

Title... _____

Author... _____

◯ Fiction: ◯ Non-Fiction:
   Genre . . . .   Subject . . . .

5	5	5	5	5	5	5	5	5	5	5	5	5	5	5	5	5	5	5	5	5	5	5	Total
5	5	5	5	5	5	5	5	5	5	5	5	5	5	5	5	5	5	5	5	5	5	5	

What I Liked About This Book...

. . . .
. . . .
. . . .
. . . .
. . . .
. . . .

I Was Really Surprised When...

. . . .
. . . .
. . . .

My Favorite Character Was...

I Liked Them Because...

. . . .

It Was Funny/Sad/Happy When They...

. . . .
. . . .
. . . .
. . . .

○ Paperback ○ Hardback ○ Ebook ○ Audiobook

Title... _____

Author... _____

○ Fiction:
Genre.................

○ Non-Fiction:
Subject..................

S	S	S	S	S	S	S	S	S	S	S	S	S	S	S	S	S	S	S	S	S	S	S	S	S	Total
S	S	S	S	S	S	S	S	S	S	S	S	S	S	S	S	S	S	S	S	S	S	S	S	S	

35

Color the stars to rate this book
1 Star = Hated it   5 Stars = Loved it

Date Started................

Date Finished................

How I Got This Book:

○ Bought it

○ Checked out from library

○ Borrowed from
....

○ Gift from:
....

This Book Was Easy To Read
○ Yes   ○ No

Stuff I Learned From This Book:
....
....
....
....
....

What I Liked About This Book...

....
....
....
....
....
....
....
....

I Was Really Surprised When...

....
....
....
....

My Favorite Character Was...

....

I Liked Them Because...

....
....

Favorite Quote From The Book:
....

It Was Funny/Sad/Happy When They...

....
....
....
....
....
....
....

○ Paperback   ○ Hardback   ○ Ebook   ○ Audiobook

36

Color the stars to rate this book
1 Star = Hated it   5 Stars = Loved it

Date Started . . . .

Date Finished . . . .

←————— // —————→

How I Got This Book:

○ Bought it

○ Checked out from library

○ Borrowed from

. . . .

○ Gift from:

. . . .

←————— // —————→

This Book Was Easy To Read
○ Yes   ○ No

←————— // —————→

Stuff I Learned From This Book:

. . . .

. . . .

. . . .

. . . .

. . . .

. . . .

Favorite Quote From The Book:

. . . .

. . . .

. . . .

. . . .

. . . .

Title... _____ ✏

Author... _____ ✏

○ Fiction: ○ Non-Fiction:
   Genre. . . . .   Subject. . . . .

S	S	S	S	S	S	S	S	S	S	S	S	S	S	S	S	S	S	S	S	S	S	S	S	S	Total
S	S	S	S	S	S	S	S	S	S	S	S	S	S	S	S	S	S	S	S	S	S	S	S	S	

What I Liked About This Book...

. . . .

. . . .

. . . .

. . . .

. . . .

. . . .

I Was Really Surprised When...

. . . .

. . . .

. . . .

My Favorite Character Was...

. . . .

I Liked Them Because...

. . . .

. . . .

It Was Funny/Sad/Happy When They...

. . . .

. . . .

. . . .

. . . .

○ Paperback ○ Hardback ○ Ebook ○ Audiobook

Title..._____

Author..._____

○ Fiction: ○ Non-Fiction:

Genre. . . . .   Subject. . . . .

5	5	5	5	5	5	5	5	5	5	5	5	5	5	5	5	5	5	5	5	5	5	5	5	Total
5	5	5	5	5	5	5	5	5	5	5	5	5	5	5	5	5	5	5	5	5	5	5	5	

37

Color the stars to rate this book
1 Star = Hated it   5 Stars = Loved it

Date Started . . . .

Date Finished. . . . .

←————————//———————→

How I Got This Book:

○ Bought it

○ Checked out from library

○ Borrowed from

. . . .

○ Gift from:

. . . .
←————————//———————→

This Book Was Easy To Read

○ Yes   ○ No
←————————//———————→

Stuff I Learned From This Book:

What I Liked About This Book...

. . . .

. . . .

. . . .

. . . .

. . . .

. . . .

. . . .

. . . .

I Was Really Surprised When...

. . . .

. . . .

. . . .

. . . .

My Favorite Character Was...

. . . .

I Liked Them Because...

. . . .

. . . .

Favorite Quote From The Book:

It Was Funny/Sad/Happy When They...

. . . .

. . . .

. . . .

. . . .

○ Paperback ○ Hardback ○ Ebook ○ Audiobook

38

Color the stars to rate this book
1 Star = Hated it   5 Stars = Loved it

Date Started . . . .

Date Finished . . . .

←————— // —————→

How I Got This Book:

○ Bought it

○ Checked out from library

○ Borrowed from

. . . .

○ Gift from:

. . . .

←————— // —————→

This Book Was Easy To Read

○ Yes   ○ No

←————— // —————→

Stuff I Learned From This Book:

. . . .

. . . .

. . . .

. . . .

. . . .

Favorite Quote From The Book:

. . . .

. . . .

. . . .

. . . .

. . . .

Title... _____

Author... _____

○ Fiction: ○ Non-Fiction:

  Genre. . . . .   Subject. . . . .

S	S	S	S	S	S	S	S	S	S	S	S	S	S	S	S	S	S	S	S	S	S	S	S	S	Total
S	S	S	S	S	S	S	S	S	S	S	S	S	S	S	S	S	S	S	S	S	S	S	S	S	

What I Liked About This Book...

. . . .

. . . .

. . . .

. . . .

. . . .

. . . .

I Was Really Surprised When...

. . . .

. . . .

. . . .

My Favorite Character Was...

. . . .

I Liked Them Because...

. . . .

. . . .

It Was Funny/Sad/Happy When They...

. . . .

. . . .

. . . .

◯ Paperback ◯ Hardback ◯ Ebook ◯ Audiobook

Title..._____

Author..._____

◯ Fiction: ◯ Non-Fiction:
   Genre. . . . .   Subject. . . . .

| 5 | 5 | 5 | 5 | 5 | 5 | 5 | 5 | 5 | 5 | 5 | 5 | 5 | 5 | 5 | 5 | 5 | 5 | 5 | 5 | 5 | 5 | 5 | 5 | Total |
| 5 | 5 | 5 | 5 | 5 | 5 | 5 | 5 | 5 | 5 | 5 | 5 | 5 | 5 | 5 | 5 | 5 | 5 | 5 | 5 | 5 | 5 | 5 | 5 | |

39

Color the stars to rate this book
I Star = Hated it   5 Stars = Loved it

What I Liked About This Book...

. . . .
. . . .
. . . .
. . . .
. . . .
. . . .
. . . .

Date Started . . . .
Date Finished . . . .
←——————//——————→
How I Got This Book:
◯ Bought it
◯ Checked out from library
◯ Borrowed from
. . . .
◯ Gift from:
. . . .
←——————//——————→

I Was Really Surprised When...

. . . .
. . . .
. . . .
. . . .

This Book Was Easy To Read
◯ Yes   ◯ No
←——————//——————→
Stuff I Learned From This Book:

. . . .

My Favorite Character Was...

. . . .

I Liked Them Because...

. . . .
. . . .

. . . .

Favorite Quote From The Book:

It Was Funny/Sad/Happy When They...

. . . .
. . . .
. . . .
. . . .

40

Color the stars to rate this book
1 Star = Hated it   5 Stars = Loved it

Date Started . . . .

Date Finished . . . .

How I Got This Book:

◌ Bought it

◌ Checked out from library

◌ Borrowed from

. . . .

◌ Gift from:

. . . .

This Book Was Easy To Read

◌ Yes   ◌ No

Stuff I Learned From This Book:

. . . .

. . . .

. . . .

. . . .

. . . .

. . . .

Favorite Quote From The Book:

. . . .

. . . .

. . . .

. . . .

. . . .

◌ Paperback   ◌ Hardback   ◌ Ebook   ◌ Audiobook

Title . . . _____ ✏

Author . . . _____ ✏

◌ Fiction: ◌ Non-Fiction:

   Genre . . . .   Subject . . . .

S	S	S	S	S	S	S	S	S	S	S	S	S	S	S	S	S	S	S	S	S	S	S	S	S	Total
S	S	S	S	S	S	S	S	S	S	S	S	S	S	S	S	S	S	S	S	S	S	S	S		

What I Liked About This Book...

. . . .

. . . .

. . . .

. . . .

. . . .

. . . .

I Was Really Surprised When...

. . . .

. . . .

. . . .

My Favorite Character Was...

I Liked Them Because...

. . . .

It Was Funny/Sad/Happy When They...

. . . .

. . . .

. . . .

◌ Paperback ◌ Hardback ◌ Ebook ◌ Audiobook

Title... _____

Author... _____

◌ Fiction: ◌ Non-Fiction:
  Genre. . . . .   Subject. . . . .

| S | S | S | S | S | S | S | S | S | S | S | S | S | S | S | S | S | S | S | S | S | S | S | S | S | S | Total |
| S | S | S | S | S | S | S | S | S | S | S | S | S | S | S | S | S | S | S | S | S | S | S | S | S | S | |

41

Color the stars to rate this book
1 Star = Hated it   5 Stars = Loved it

What I Liked About This Book...

. . . .
. . . .
. . . .
. . . .
. . . .
. . . .
. . . .

Date Started . . . .
Date Finished. . . . .

How I Got This Book:
◌ Bought it
◌ Checked out from library
◌ Borrowed from
  . . . .
◌ Gift from:
  . . . .

I Was Really Surprised When...

. . . .
. . . .
. . . .
. . . .

This Book Was Easy To Read
◌ Yes   ◌ No

Stuff I Learned From This Book:
. . . .
. . . .

My Favorite Character Was...

. . . .

I Liked Them Because...

. . . .
. . . .

. . . .

Favorite Quote From The Book:

It Was Funny/Sad/Happy When They...

. . . .
. . . .
. . . .
. . . .

. . . .
. . . .

42

Color the stars to rate this book
1 Star = Hated it   5 Stars = Loved it

Date Started . . . .

Date Finished . . . .

How I Got This Book:

○ Bought it

○ Checked out from library

○ Borrowed from

. . . .

○ Gift from:

. . . .

This Book Was Easy To Read

○ Yes   ○ No

Stuff I Learned From This Book:

. . . .

. . . .

. . . .

. . . .

. . . .

Favorite Quote From The Book:

. . . .

. . . .

. . . .

. . . .

. . . .

○ Paperback   ○ Hardback   ○ Ebook   ○ Audiobook

Title . . . _____

Author . . . _____

○ Fiction: ○ Non-Fiction:

  Genre . . . .   Subject . . . .

5	5	5	5	5	5	5	5	5	5	5	5	5	5	5	5	5	5	5	5	5	5	5	5	Total
5	5	5	5	5	5	5	5	5	5	5	5	5	5	5	5	5	5	5	5	5	5	5	5	

What I Liked About This Book...

. . . .

. . . .

. . . .

. . . .

. . . .

. . . .

I Was Really Surprised When...

. . . .

. . . .

. . . .

My Favorite Character Was...

. . . .

I Liked Them Because...

. . . .

. . . .

It Was Funny/Sad/Happy When They...

. . . .

. . . .

. . . .

○ Paperback ○ Hardback ○ Ebook ○ Audiobook

Title..._____

Author..._____

○ Fiction: ○ Non-Fiction:

Genre................   Subject................

5	5	5	5	5	5	5	5	5	5	5	5	5	5	5	5	5	5	5	5	5	5	5	5	5	Total
5	5	5	5	5	5	5	5	5	5	5	5	5	5	5	5	5	5	5	5	5	5	5	5	5	

43

Color the stars to rate this book
1 Star = Hated it   5 Stars = Loved it

What I Liked About This Book...

....
....
....
....
....
....
....
....

I Was Really Surprised When...

....
....
....
....

My Favorite Character Was...

....

I Liked Them Because...

....
....

It Was Funny/Sad/Happy When They...

....
....
....
....

Date Started................

Date Finished................

How I Got This Book:

○ Bought it

○ Checked out from library

○ Borrowed from

....

○ Gift from:

....

This Book Was Easy To Read

○ Yes   ○ No

Stuff I Learned From This Book:

....
....
....
....
....

Favorite Quote From The Book:

....
....
....
....

44

Color the stars to rate this book
1 Star = Hated it   5 Stars = Loved it

Date Started . . . .

Date Finished . . . .

How I Got This Book:

◯ Bought it

◯ Checked out from library

◯ Borrowed from

. . . .

◯ Gift from:

. . . .

This Book Was Easy To Read

◯ Yes   ◯ No

Stuff I Learned From This Book:

. . . .

. . . .

. . . .

. . . .

. . . .

. . . .

Favorite Quote From The Book:

. . . .

. . . .

. . . .

. . . .

◯ Paperback ◯ Hardback ◯ Ebook ◯ Audiobook

Title . . . _____

Author . . . _____

◯ Fiction: ◯ Non-Fiction:
   Genre . . . .   Subject . . . .

5	5	5	5	5	5	5	5	5	5	5	5	5	5	5	5	5	5	5	5	5	5	5	5	5	Total
5	5	5	5	5	5	5	5	5	5	5	5	5	5	5	5	5	5	5	5	5	5	5	5	5	

What I Liked About This Book...

. . . .

. . . .

. . . .

. . . .

. . . .

. . . .

I Was Really Surprised When...

. . . .

. . . .

. . . .

My Favorite Character Was...

I Liked Them Because...

. . . .

. . . .

It Was Funny/Sad/Happy When They...

. . . .

. . . .

. . . .

. . . .

◯ Paperback ◯ Hardback ◯ Ebook ◯ Audiobook

Title..._____

Author.._____

◯ Fiction: ◯ Non-Fiction:
  Genre...................   Subject................

| S | S | S | S | S | S | S | S | S | S | S | S | S | S | S | S | S | S | S | S | S | S | S | S | S | S | S | Total |
| S | S | S | S | S | S | S | S | S | S | S | S | S | S | S | S | S | S | S | S | S | S | S | S | S | S | S | |

45

Color the stars to rate this book
1 Star = Hated it   5 Stars = Loved it

What I Liked About This Book...

....
....
....
....
....
....
....
....

Date Started ....
Date Finished................
←————//————→
How I Got This Book:
◯ Bought it
◯ Checked out from library
◯ Borrowed from

....
◯ Gift from:

....
←————//————→
This Book Was Easy To Read
◯ Yes   ◯ No
←————//————→
Stuff I Learned From This Book:

I Was Really Surprised When...

....
....
....

....
....
....
....

My Favorite Character Was...

I Liked Them Because...

....
....

....

Favorite Quote From The Book:

It Was Funny/Sad/Happy When They...

....
....
....
....

....
....
....
....
....

46

Color the stars to rate this book
1 Star = Hated it   5 Stars = Loved it

Date Started . . . .

Date Finished . . . .

How I Got This Book:

○ Bought it

○ Checked out from library

○ Borrowed from

. . . .

○ Gift from:

. . . .

This Book Was Easy To Read

○ Yes   ○ No

Stuff I Learned From This Book:

. . . .

. . . .

. . . .

. . . .

. . . .

. . . .

Favorite Quote From The Book:

. . . .

. . . .

. . . .

. . . .

Title . . . _____ ✏

Author . . . _____ ✏

○ Fiction: ○ Non-Fiction:

  Genre . . . .   Subject . . . .

5	5	5	5	5	5	5	5	5	5	5	5	5	5	5	5	5	5	5	5	5	5	5	Total
5	5	5	5	5	5	5	5	5	5	5	5	5	5	5	5	5	5	5	5	5	5	5	

What I Liked About This Book...

. . . .

. . . .

. . . .

. . . .

. . . .

. . . .

. . . .

I Was Really Surprised When...

. . . .

. . . .

. . . .

My Favorite Character Was...

. . . .

I Liked Them Because...

. . . .

. . . .

It Was Funny/Sad/Happy When They...

. . . .

. . . .

. . . .

◯ Paperback   ◯ Hardback   ◯ Ebook   ◯ Audiobook

Title..._____

Author..._____

◯ Fiction: ◯ Non-Fiction:
   Genre............   Subject.................

5	5	5	5	5	5	5	5	5	5	5	5	5	5	5	5	5	5	5	5	5	5	5	5	5	Total
5	5	5	5	5	5	5	5	5	5	5	5	5	5	5	5	5	5	5	5	5	5	5	5	5	

What I Liked About This Book...

....
....
....
....
....
....
....

I Was Really Surprised When...

....
....
....

My Favorite Character Was...

I Liked Them Because...

....
....

It Was Funny/Sad/Happy When They...

....
....
....
....

47

Color the stars to rate this book
1 Star = Hated it   5 Stars = Loved it

Date Started...............

Date Finished...............

How I Got This Book:
◯ Bought it
◯ Checked out from library
◯ Borrowed from
   ....
◯ Gift from:
   ....

This Book Was Easy To Read
◯ Yes   ◯ No

Stuff I Learned From This Book:
....
....
....
....
....

Favorite Quote From The Book:
....
....

○ Paperback ○ Hardback ○ Ebook ○ Audiobook

48

Color the stars to rate this book
1 Star = Hated it   5 Stars = Loved it

Date Started . . . .

Date Finished . . . .

⟵————//————⟶

How I Got This Book:

○ Bought it

○ Checked out from library

○ Borrowed from

. . . .

○ Gift from:

. . . .

⟵————//————⟶

This Book Was Easy To Read

○ Yes   ○ No

⟵————//————⟶

Stuff I Learned From This Book:

. . . .

. . . .

. . . .

. . . .

. . . .

. . . .

Favorite Quote From The Book:

. . . .

. . . .

. . . .

. . . .

. . . .

Title... _____ ✏

Author... _____ ✏

○ Fiction: ○ Non-Fiction:

Genre. . . . .   Subject. . . . .

5	5	5	5	5	5	5	5	5	5	5	5	5	5	5	5	5	5	5	5	5	5	5	5	Total
5	5	5	5	5	5	5	5	5	5	5	5	5	5	5	5	5	5	5	5	5	5	5	5	

What I Liked About This Book...

. . . .

. . . .

. . . .

. . . .

. . . .

. . . .

I Was Really Surprised When...

. . . .

. . . .

. . . .

My Favorite Character Was...

I Liked Them Because...

. . . .

. . . .

It Was Funny/Sad/Happy When They...

. . . .

. . . .

. . . .

. . . .

○ Paperback ○ Hardback ○ Ebook ○ Audiobook

Title..._____

Author..._____

○ Fiction: ○ Non-Fiction:
  Genre.............   Subject...............

5	5	5	5	5	5	5	5	5	5	5	5	5	5	5	5	5	5	5	5	5	5	5	5	5	Total
5	5	5	5	5	5	5	5	5	5	5	5	5	5	5	5	5	5	5	5	5	5	5	5	5	

What I Liked About This Book...

....
....
....
....
....
....
....

I Was Really Surprised When...

....
....
....
....

My Favorite Character Was...

I Liked Them Because...

....
....
....

It Was Funny/Sad/Happy When They...

....
....
....
....

49

Color the stars to rate this book
1 Star = Hated it   5 Stars = Loved it

Date Started ....

Date Finished...............

←————//————→

How I Got This Book:
○ Bought it
○ Checked out from library
○ Borrowed from
  ....
○ Gift from:
  ....

←————//————→

This Book Was Easy To Read
○ Yes   ○ No

←————//————→

Stuff I Learned From This Book:

....
....
....
....
....
....

Favorite Quote From The Book:

....
....
....

○ Paperback ○ Hardback ○ Ebook ○ Audiobook

50

Color the stars to rate this book
1 Star = Hated it   5 Stars = Loved it

Date Started . . . .

Date Finished . . . .

←————— // ————→

How I Got This Book:

○ Bought it

○ Checked out from library

○ Borrowed from
. . . .

○ Gift from:
. . . .

←————— // ————→

This Book Was Easy To Read
○ Yes   ○ No

←————— // ————→

Stuff I Learned From This Book:

. . . .
. . . .
. . . .
. . . .
. . . .
. . . .

Favorite Quote From The Book:

. . . .
. . . .
. . . .
. . . .

Title . . _____ ✎

Author . . _____ ✎

○ Fiction: ○ Non-Fiction:
   Genre . . . .   Subject . . . .

5	5	5	5	5	5	5	5	5	5	5	5	5	5	5	5	5	5	5	5	5	5	5	Total
5	5	5	5	5	5	5	5	5	5	5	5	5	5	5	5	5	5	5	5	5	5	5	

What I Liked About This Book...

. . . .
. . . .
. . . .
. . . .
. . . .
. . . .
. . . .

I Was Really Surprised When...

. . . .
. . . .
. . . .

My Favorite Character Was...

I Liked Them Because...

. . . .

It Was Funny/Sad/Happy When They...

. . . .
. . . .
. . . .

○ Paperback ○ Hardback ○ Ebook ○ Audiobook

Title..._____

Author..._____

○ Fiction: ○ Non-Fiction:
  Genre..................   Subject................

5	5	5	5	5	5	5	5	5	5	5	5	5	5	5	5	5	5	5	5	5	5	5	5	5	5	5	Total
5	5	5	5	5	5	5	5	5	5	5	5	5	5	5	5	5	5	5	5	5	5	5	5	5	5	5	

51

Color the stars to rate this book
1 Star = Hated it   5 Stars = Loved it

Date Started................
Date Finished................
←————//————→
How I Got This Book:
○ Bought it
○ Checked out from library
○ Borrowed from
....
○ Gift from:
....
←————//————→
This Book Was Easy To Read
○ Yes   ○ No
←————//————→

What I Liked About This Book...
....
....
....
....
....
....
....

I Was Really Surprised When...
....
....
....

Stuff I Learned From This Book:
....
....
....
....

My Favorite Character Was...
....

I Liked Them Because...
....
....

....

Favorite Quote From The Book:
....

It Was Funny/Sad/Happy When They...
....
....
....
....

○ Paperback ○ Hardback ○ Ebook ○ Audiobook

52

Color the stars to rate this book
1 Star = Hated it   5 Stars = Loved it

Date Started . . . .

Date Finished . . . .

How I Got This Book:

○ Bought it

○ Checked out from library

○ Borrowed from

. . . .

○ Gift from:

. . . .

This Book Was Easy To Read
○ Yes   ○ No

Stuff I Learned From This Book:

. . . .

. . . .

. . . .

. . . .

. . . .

. . . .

. . . .

Favorite Quote From The Book:

. . . .

. . . .

. . . .

. . . .

. . . .

Title... _____

Author... _____

○ Fiction: ○ Non-Fiction:
   Genre. . . . .   Subject. . . . .

5	5	5	5	5	5	5	5	5	5	5	5	5	5	5	5	5	5	5	5	5	5	5	Total
5	5	5	5	5	5	5	5	5	5	5	5	5	5	5	5	5	5	5	5	5	5	5	

What I Liked About This Book...

. . . .

. . . .

. . . .

. . . .

. . . .

. . . .

. . . .

I Was Really Surprised When...

. . . .

. . . .

. . . .

My Favorite Character Was...

I Liked Them Because...

. . . .

. . . .

It Was Funny/Sad/Happy When They...

. . . .

. . . .

. . . .

. . . .

◯ Paperback ◯ Hardback ◯ Ebook ◯ Audiobook

Title.._____ 🖉

Author.._____ 🖉

◯ Fiction: ◯ Non-Fiction:
   Genre. . . . .   Subject. . . . .

5	5	5	5	5	5	5	5	5	5	5	5	5	5	5	5	5	5	5	5	5	5	5	5	5	5	Total
5	5	5	5	5	5	5	5	5	5	5	5	5	5	5	5	5	5	5	5	5	5	5	5	5	5	

53

Color the stars to rate this book
1 Star = Hated it   5 Stars = Loved it

What I Liked About This Book...

. . . .
. . . .
. . . .
. . . .
. . . .
. . . .

Date Started . . . .
Date Finished. . . . .
←————————//————————→
How I Got This Book:
◯ Bought it
◯ Checked out from library
◯ Borrowed from
   . . . .
◯ Gift from:
   . . . .
←————————//————————→
This Book Was Easy To Read
◯ Yes   ◯ No
←————————//————————→
Stuff I Learned From This Book:

I Was Really Surprised When...

. . . .
. . . .
. . . .

. . . .
. . . .
. . . .

My Favorite Character Was...

. . . .

I Liked Them Because...

. . . .
. . . .

. . . .

Favorite Quote From The Book:

It Was Funny/Sad/Happy When They...

. . . .
. . . .
. . . .
. . . .

. . . .
. . . .
. . . .

○ Paperback   ○ Hardback   ○ Ebook   ○ Audiobook

54

Color the stars to rate this book
I Star = Hated it   5 Stars = Loved it

Date Started . . . .

Date Finished . . . .

⟵————— // —————⟶

How I Got This Book:

○ Bought it

○ Checked out from library

○ Borrowed from

. . . .

○ Gift from:

. . . .

⟵————— // —————⟶

This Book Was Easy To Read

○ Yes   ○ No

⟵————— // —————⟶

Stuff I Learned From This Book:

. . . .

. . . .

. . . .

. . . .

. . . .

. . . .

. . . .

Favorite Quote From The Book:

. . . .

. . . .

. . . .

. . . .

. . . .

Title... _____

Author... _____

○ Fiction: ○ Non-Fiction:
  Genre. . . . .   Subject. . . . .

5	5	5	5	5	5	5	5	5	5	5	5	5	5	5	5	5	5	5	5	5	5	5	5	Total
5	5	5	5	5	5	5	5	5	5	5	5	5	5	5	5	5	5	5	5	5	5	5	5	

What I Liked About This Book...

. . . .

. . . .

. . . .

. . . .

. . . .

. . . .

. . . .

I Was Really Surprised When...

. . . .

. . . .

. . . .

My Favorite Character Was...

I Liked Them Because...

. . . .

. . . .

It Was Funny/Sad/Happy When They...

. . . .

. . . .

. . . .

. . . .

○ Paperback ○ Hardback ○ Ebook ○ Audiobook

Title..._____

Author.._____

○ Fiction: ○ Non-Fiction:
   Genre. . . . .   Subject. . . . .

| 5 | 5 | 5 | 5 | 5 | 5 | 5 | 5 | 5 | 5 | 5 | 5 | 5 | 5 | 5 | 5 | 5 | 5 | 5 | 5 | 5 | 5 | 5 | 5 | 5 | Total |
| 5 | 5 | 5 | 5 | 5 | 5 | 5 | 5 | 5 | 5 | 5 | 5 | 5 | 5 | 5 | 5 | 5 | 5 | 5 | 5 | 5 | 5 | 5 | 5 | 5 | |

55

Color the stars to rate this book
1 Star = Hated it   5 Stars = Loved it

What I Liked About This Book...

. . . .
. . . .
. . . .
. . . .
. . . .
. . . .
. . . .

Date Started . . . .
Date Finished . . . .
←————————//————————→
How I Got This Book:
○ Bought it
○ Checked out from library
○ Borrowed from
   . . . .
○ Gift from:
   . . . .
←————————//————————→
This Book Was Easy To Read
○ Yes   ○ No
←————————//————————→
Stuff I Learned From This Book:
. . . .
. . . .
. . . .
. . . .
. . . .

I Was Really Surprised When...

. . . .
. . . .
. . . .
. . . .

My Favorite Character Was...

. . . .

I Liked Them Because...

. . . .
. . . .

Favorite Quote From The Book:
. . . .

It Was Funny/Sad/Happy When They...

. . . .
. . . .
. . . .
. . . .

○ Paperback ○ Hardback ○ Ebook ○ Audiobook

56

Color the stars to rate this book
1 Star = Hated it   5 Stars = Loved it

Date Started . . . .

Date Finished . . . .

←——————— // ———————→

How I Got This Book:

○ Bought it

○ Checked out from library

○ Borrowed from

. . . .

○ Gift from:

←——————— // ———————→

This Book Was Easy To Read
○ Yes   ○ No

←——————— // ———————→

Stuff I Learned From This Book:

. . . .

. . . .

. . . .

. . . .

. . . .

. . . .

Favorite Quote From The Book:

. . . .

. . . .

. . . .

. . . .

. . . .

Title... _____

Author... _____

○ Fiction: ○ Non-Fiction:
   Genre. . . . .   Subject. . . . .

5	5	5	5	5	5	5	5	5	5	5	5	5	5	5	5	5	5	5	5	5	5	5	5	5	Total
5	5	5	5	5	5	5	5	5	5	5	5	5	5	5	5	5	5	5	5	5	5	5	5	5	

What I Liked About This Book...

. . . .

. . . .

. . . .

. . . .

. . . .

. . . .

. . . .

I Was Really Surprised When...

. . . .

. . . .

. . . .

My Favorite Character Was...

I Liked Them Because...

. . . .

. . . .

It Was Funny/Sad/Happy When They...

. . . .

. . . .

. . . .

. . . .

○ Paperback ○ Hardback ○ Ebook ○ Audiobook

Title..._____

Author..._____

○ Fiction: ○ Non-Fiction:
  Genre. . . . .   Subject. . . . .

| 5 | 5 | 5 | 5 | 5 | 5 | 5 | 5 | 5 | 5 | 5 | 5 | 5 | 5 | 5 | 5 | 5 | 5 | 5 | 5 | 5 | 5 | 5 | 5 | 5 | 5 | Total |
| 5 | 5 | 5 | 5 | 5 | 5 | 5 | 5 | 5 | 5 | 5 | 5 | 5 | 5 | 5 | 5 | 5 | 5 | 5 | 5 | 5 | 5 | 5 | 5 | 5 | 5 | |

57

Color the stars to rate this book
1 Star = Hated it   5 Stars = Loved it

What I Liked About This Book...

. . . .
. . . .
. . . .
. . . .
. . . .
. . . .

Date Started . . . .

Date Finished . . . .

How I Got This Book:

○ Bought it

○ Checked out from library

○ Borrowed from

. . . .

○ Gift from:

. . . .

I Was Really Surprised When...

. . . .
. . . .
. . . .
. . . .

This Book Was Easy To Read
○ Yes   ○ No

Stuff I Learned From This Book:

. . . .

My Favorite Character Was...

. . . .

I Liked Them Because...

. . . .
. . . .

. . . .

Favorite Quote From The Book:

It Was Funny/Sad/Happy When They...

. . . .
. . . .
. . . .

. . . .

○ Paperback ○ Hardback ○ Ebook ○ Audiobook

58

Color the stars to rate this book
1 Star = Hated it   5 Stars = Loved it

Date Started . . . .

Date Finished . . . .

←——————//——————→

How I Got This Book:

○ Bought it

○ Checked out from library

○ Borrowed from

. . . .

○ Gift from:

. . . .

←——————//——————→

This Book Was Easy To Read

○ Yes   ○ No

←——————//——————→

Stuff I Learned From This Book:

. . . .

. . . .

. . . .

. . . .

. . . .

Favorite Quote From The Book:

. . . .

. . . .

. . . .

. . . .

. . . .

Title... _____

Author... _____

○ Fiction: ○ Non-Fiction:

   Genre. . . . .   Subject. . . . .

5	5	5	5	5	5	5	5	5	5	5	5	5	5	5	5	5	5	5	5	5	5	5	Total
5	5	5	5	5	5	5	5	5	5	5	5	5	5	5	5	5	5	5	5	5	5	5	

What I Liked About This Book...

. . . .

. . . .

. . . .

. . . .

. . . .

. . . .

I Was Really Surprised When...

. . . .

. . . .

. . . .

My Favorite Character Was...

I Liked Them Because...

. . . .

. . . .

It Was Funny/Sad/Happy When They...

. . . .

. . . .

. . . .

. . . .

○ Paperback ○ Hardback ○ Ebook ○ Audiobook

Title..._____

Author..._____

○ Fiction: ○ Non-Fiction:
   Genre.....................   Subject..................

5	5	5	5	5	5	5	5	5	5	5	5	5	5	5	5	5	5	5	5	5	5	5	5	5	Total
5	5	5	5	5	5	5	5	5	5	5	5	5	5	5	5	5	5	5	5	5	5	5	5	5	

59

Color the stars to rate this book
1 Star = Hated it   5 Stars = Loved it

What I Liked About This Book...

....
....
....
....
....
....

I Was Really Surprised When...

....
....
....
....

My Favorite Character Was...

I Liked Them Because...

....
....
....

It Was Funny/Sad/Happy When They...

....
....
....
....

Date Started ....
Date Finished................
←————//————→
How I Got This Book:
○ Bought it
○ Checked out from library
○ Borrowed from
....
○ Gift from:
....
←————//————→
This Book Was Easy To Read
○ Yes   ○ No
←————//————→
Stuff I Learned From This Book:
....
....
....
....
....
....
Favorite Quote From The Book:
....
....
....
....

○ Paperback   ○ Hardback   ○ Ebook   ○ Audiobook

60

Color the stars to rate this book
1 Star = Hated it   5 Stars = Loved it

Date Started . . . .

Date Finished . . . .

How I Got This Book:

○ Bought it

○ Checked out from library

○ Borrowed from

. . . .

○ Gift from:

. . . .

This Book Was Easy To Read

○ Yes   ○ No

Stuff I Learned From This Book:

. . . .

. . . .

. . . .

. . . .

. . . .

. . . .

Favorite Quote From The Book:

. . . .

. . . .

. . . .

. . . .

. . . .

Title . . . _____

Author . . . _____

○ Fiction: ○ Non-Fiction:
  Genre . . . .   Subject . . . .

| 5 | 5 | 5 | 5 | 5 | 5 | 5 | 5 | 5 | 5 | 5 | 5 | 5 | 5 | 5 | 5 | 5 | 5 | 5 | 5 | 5 | 5 | 5 | 5 | Total |
| 5 | 5 | 5 | 5 | 5 | 5 | 5 | 5 | 5 | 5 | 5 | 5 | 5 | 5 | 5 | 5 | 5 | 5 | 5 | 5 | 5 | 5 | 5 | 5 | |

What I Liked About This Book...

. . . .

. . . .

. . . .

. . . .

. . . .

. . . .

I Was Really Surprised When...

. . . .

. . . .

. . . .

My Favorite Character Was...

I Liked Them Because...

. . . .

It Was Funny/Sad/Happy When They...

. . . .

. . . .

. . . .

○ Paperback ○ Hardback ○ Ebook ○ Audiobook

Title..._____ ✏

Author..._____ ✏

○ Fiction: ○ Non-Fiction:
   Genre. . . . .   Subject. . . . .

| 5 | 5 | 5 | 5 | 5 | 5 | 5 | 5 | 5 | 5 | 5 | 5 | 5 | 5 | 5 | 5 | 5 | 5 | 5 | 5 | 5 | 5 | 5 | 5 | 5 | 5 | 5 | 5 | Total |
| 5 | 5 | 5 | 5 | 5 | 5 | 5 | 5 | 5 | 5 | 5 | 5 | 5 | 5 | 5 | 5 | 5 | 5 | 5 | 5 | 5 | 5 | 5 | 5 | 5 | 5 | 5 | 5 | |

61

Color the stars to rate this book
1 Star = Hated it   5 Stars = Loved it

What I Liked About This Book...

. . . .
. . . .
. . . .
. . . .
. . . .
. . . .
. . . .

Date Started . . . .

Date Finished . . . .

←——————— // ———————→

How I Got This Book:

○ Bought it

○ Checked out from library

○ Borrowed from

. . . .

○ Gift from:

. . . .

←——————— // ———————→

This Book Was Easy To Read
○ Yes   ○ No

←——————— // ———————→

Stuff I Learned From This Book:

I Was Really Surprised When...

. . . .
. . . .
. . . .
. . . .

. . . .
. . . .
. . . .

My Favorite Character Was...

. . . .

I Liked Them Because...

. . . .
. . . .

Favorite Quote From The Book:

. . . .

It Was Funny/Sad/Happy When They...

. . . .
. . . .
. . . .
. . . .

○ Paperback ○ Hardback ○ Ebook ○ Audiobook

62

Color the stars to rate this book
1 Star = Hated it   5 Stars = Loved it

Date Started . . . .

Date Finished . . . .

How I Got This Book:

○ Bought it

○ Checked out from library

○ Borrowed from

. . . .

○ Gift from:

. . . .

This Book Was Easy To Read

○ Yes   ○ No

Stuff I Learned From This Book:

. . . .

. . . .

. . . .

. . . .

. . . .

. . . .

. . . .

Favorite Quote From The Book:

. . . .

. . . .

. . . .

. . . .

. . . .

Title... _____ ✏

Author... _____ ✏

○ Fiction: ○ Non-Fiction:
   Genre. . . . .   Subject. . . . .

5	5	5	5	5	5	5	5	5	5	5	5	5	5	5	5	5	5	5	5	5	5	5	5	Total
5	5	5	5	5	5	5	5	5	5	5	5	5	5	5	5	5	5	5	5	5	5	5	5	

What I Liked About This Book...

. . . .

. . . .

. . . .

. . . .

. . . .

. . . .

I Was Really Surprised When...

. . . .

. . . .

. . . .

My Favorite Character Was...

I Liked Them Because...

. . . .

. . . .

It Was Funny/Sad/Happy When They...

. . . .

. . . .

. . . .

. . . .

◯ Paperback ◯ Hardback ◯ Ebook ◯ Audiobook

Title..._____

Author..._____

◯ Fiction: ◯ Non-Fiction:
  Genre............   Subject................

| 5 | 5 | 5 | 5 | 5 | 5 | 5 | 5 | 5 | 5 | 5 | 5 | 5 | 5 | 5 | 5 | 5 | 5 | 5 | 5 | 5 | 5 | 5 | 5 | 5 | Total |
| 5 | 5 | 5 | 5 | 5 | 5 | 5 | 5 | 5 | 5 | 5 | 5 | 5 | 5 | 5 | 5 | 5 | 5 | 5 | 5 | 5 | 5 | 5 | 5 | 5 | |

What I Liked About This Book...

....
....
....
....
....
....
....

I Was Really Surprised When...

....
....
....
....

My Favorite Character Was...

....

I Liked Them Because...

....
....

It Was Funny/Sad/Happy When They...

....
....
....
....

63

Color the stars to rate this book
1 Star = Hated it   5 Stars = Loved it

Date Started ....
Date Finished................

How I Got This Book:
◯ Bought it
◯ Checked out from library
◯ Borrowed from
  ....
◯ Gift from:
  ....

This Book Was Easy To Read
◯ Yes   ◯ No

Stuff I Learned From This Book:
....
....
....
....
....

Favorite Quote From The Book:
....
....
....
....

○ Paperback ○ Hardback ○ Ebook ○ Audiobook

64

Color the stars to rate this book
1 Star = Hated it   5 Stars = Loved it

Date Started . . . .

Date Finished . . . .

←————————// ————————→

How I Got This Book:

○ Bought it

○ Checked out from library

○ Borrowed from

. . . .

○ Gift from:

. . . .

←————————// ————————→

This Book Was Easy To Read
○ Yes   ○ No

←————————// ————————→

Stuff I Learned From This Book:

. . . .

. . . .

. . . .

. . . .

. . . .

. . . .

Favorite Quote From The Book:

. . . .

. . . .

. . . .

. . . .

. . . .

Title... _____

Author... _____

○ Fiction: ○ Non-Fiction:
  Genre. . . . .   Subject. . . . .

5	5	5	5	5	5	5	5	5	5	5	5	5	5	5	5	5	5	5	5	5	5	5	5	Total
5	5	5	5	5	5	5	5	5	5	5	5	5	5	5	5	5	5	5	5	5	5	5	5	

What I Liked About This Book...

. . . .

. . . .

. . . .

. . . .

. . . .

. . . .

. . . .

I Was Really Surprised When...

. . . .

. . . .

. . . .

My Favorite Character Was...

I Liked Them Because...

. . . .

. . . .

It Was Funny/Sad/Happy When They...

. . . .

. . . .

. . . .

. . . .

○ Paperback ○ Hardback ○ Ebook ○ Audiobook

Title..._____

Author..._____

○ Fiction: ○ Non-Fiction:
  Genre. . . . .   Subject. . . . .

5	5	5	5	5	5	5	5	5	5	5	5	5	5	5	5	5	5	5	5	5	5	5	5	5	5	5	Total
5	5	5	5	5	5	5	5	5	5	5	5	5	5	5	5	5	5	5	5	5	5	5	5	5	5	5	

65

Color the stars to rate this book
1 Star = Hated it   5 Stars = Loved it

What I Liked About This Book...
. . . .
. . . .
. . . .
. . . .
. . . .
. . . .
. . . .

Date Started . . . .
Date Finished . . . .
←————————//————————→
How I Got This Book:
○ Bought it
○ Checked out from library
○ Borrowed from
. . . .
○ Gift from:
. . . .
←————————//————————→

I Was Really Surprised When...
. . . .
. . . .
. . . .
. . . .

This Book Was Easy To Read
○ Yes   ○ No
←————————//————————→
Stuff I Learned From This Book:
. . . .
. . . .
. . . .

My Favorite Character Was...
. . . .

I Liked Them Because...
. . . .
. . . .

Favorite Quote From The Book:
. . . .

It Was Funny/Sad/Happy When They...
. . . .
. . . .
. . . .
. . . .

66

Color the stars to rate this book
I Star = Hated it   5 Stars = Loved it

Date Started . . . .

Date Finished . . . .

←———————//———————→

How I Got This Book:

○ Bought it

○ Checked out from library

○ Borrowed from

. . . .

○ Gift from:

. . . .

←———————//———————→

This Book Was Easy To Read
○ Yes   ○ No
←———————//———————→

Stuff I Learned From This Book:

. . . .

. . . .

. . . .

. . . .

. . . .

Favorite Quote From The Book:

. . . .

. . . .

. . . .

. . . .

. . . .

Title... _____ ✐

Author... _____ ✐

○ Fiction: ○ Non-Fiction:

    Genre. . . . .   Subject. . . . .

5	5	5	5	5	5	5	5	5	5	5	5	5	5	5	5	5	5	5	5	5	5	Total
5	5	5	5	5	5	5	5	5	5	5	5	5	5	5	5	5	5	5	5	5	5	

What I Liked About This Book...

. . . .

. . . .

. . . .

. . . .

. . . .

. . . .

. . . .

I Was Really Surprised When...

. . . .

. . . .

. . . .

My Favorite Character Was...

I Liked Them Because...

. . . .

. . . .

It Was Funny/Sad/Happy When They...

. . . .

. . . .

. . . .

. . . .

○ Paperback ○ Hardback ○ Ebook ○ Audiobook

Title..._____ ✎

Author..._____ ✎

○ Fiction: ○ Non-Fiction:
  Genre. . . . .   Subject. . . . .

| S | S | S | S | S | S | S | S | S | S | S | S | S | S | S | S | S | S | S | S | S | S | S | S | S | S | S | Total |
| S | S | S | S | S | S | S | S | S | S | S | S | S | S | S | S | S | S | S | S | S | S | S | S | S | S | S | |

67

Color the stars to rate this book
1 Star = Hated it   5 Stars = Loved it

What I Liked About This Book...

. . . .
. . . .
. . . .
. . . .
. . . .
. . . .
. . . .
. . . .

Date Started . . . .

Date Finished. . . . .

How I Got This Book:

○ Bought it

○ Checked out from library

○ Borrowed from

. . . .

○ Gift from:

. . . .

I Was Really Surprised When...

. . . .
. . . .
. . . .
. . . .

This Book Was Easy To Read
○ Yes   ○ No

Stuff I Learned From This Book:

. . . .

. . . .

My Favorite Character Was...

. . . .

I Liked Them Because...

. . . .
. . . .

. . . .

. . . .

Favorite Quote From The Book:

It Was Funny/Sad/Happy When They...

. . . .
. . . .
. . . .
. . . .

. . . .

○ Paperback   ○ Hardback   ○ Ebook   ○ Audiobook

Color the stars to rate this book
1 Star = Hated it   5 Stars = Loved it

Title..._____

Author.._____

○ Fiction: ○ Non-Fiction:
   Genre. . . . .   Subject. . . . .

Date Started . . . .

Date Finished. . . . .

5	5	5	5	5	5	5	5	5	5	5	5	5	5	5	5	5	5	5	5	5	5	5	5	Total
5	5	5	5	5	5	5	5	5	5	5	5	5	5	5	5	5	5	5	5	5	5	5	5	

<——————— // ———————>

How I Got This Book:

○ Bought it

○ Checked out from library

○ Borrowed from

. . . .

○ Gift from:

. . . .

<——————— // ———————>

This Book Was Easy To Read

○ Yes   ○ No

<——————— // ———————>

Stuff I Learned From This Book:

. . . .

. . . .

. . . .

. . . .

. . . .

. . . .

Favorite Quote From The Book:

. . . .

. . . .

. . . .

. . . .

. . . .

What I Liked About This Book...

. . . .

. . . .

. . . .

. . . .

. . . .

. . . .

I Was Really Surprised When...

. . . .

. . . .

. . . .

My Favorite Character Was...

I Liked Them Because...

. . . .

. . . .

It Was Funny/Sad/Happy When They...

. . . .

. . . .

. . . .

◯ Paperback ◯ Hardback ◯ Ebook ◯ Audiobook

Title... _____

Author... _____

◯ Fiction:
Genre. . . . .

◯ Non-Fiction:
Subject. . . . .

5	5	5	5	5	5	5	5	5	5	5	5	5	5	5	5	5	5	5	5	5	5	5	5	5	Total
5	5	5	5	5	5	5	5	5	5	5	5	5	5	5	5	5	5	5	5	5	5	5	5	5	

69

Color the stars to rate this book
1 Star = Hated it   5 Stars = Loved it

Date Started . . . .

Date Finished. . . . .

←————————//————————→

How I Got This Book:

◯ Bought it

◯ Checked out from library

◯ Borrowed from

. . . .

◯ Gift from:

. . . .

←————————//————————→

This Book Was Easy To Read
◯ Yes   ◯ No

←————————//————————→

What I Liked About This Book...

. . . .
. . . .
. . . .
. . . .
. . . .
. . . .

Stuff I Learned From This Book:

. . . .

I Was Really Surprised When...

. . . .
. . . .
. . . .

. . . .

My Favorite Character Was...

. . . .

I Liked Them Because...

. . . .
. . . .

Favorite Quote From The Book:

It Was Funny/Sad/Happy When They...

. . . .
. . . .
. . . .
. . . .

70

Color the stars to rate this book
1 Star = Hated it   5 Stars = Loved it

Date Started . . . .

Date Finished . . . .

←————————//————→

How I Got This Book:

○ Bought it

○ Checked out from library

○ Borrowed from

. . . .

○ Gift from:

. . . .

←————————//————→

This Book Was Easy To Read

○ Yes   ○ No

←————————//————→

Stuff I Learned From This Book:

. . . .

. . . .

. . . .

. . . .

. . . .

. . . .

Favorite Quote From The Book:

. . . .

. . . .

. . . .

. . . .

Title... _____

Author... _____

○ Fiction: ○ Non-Fiction:

   Genre. . . . .   Subject. . . . .

5	5	5	5	5	5	5	5	5	5	5	5	5	5	5	5	5	5	5	5	5	5	5	5	Total
5	5	5	5	5	5	5	5	5	5	5	5	5	5	5	5	5	5	5	5	5	5	5	5	

What I Liked About This Book...

. . . .

. . . .

. . . .

. . . .

. . . .

. . . .

. . . .

I Was Really Surprised When...

. . . .

. . . .

. . . .

My Favorite Character Was...

I Liked Them Because...

. . . .

. . . .

It Was Funny/Sad/Happy When They...

. . . .

. . . .

. . . .

. . . .

○ Paperback ○ Hardback ○ Ebook ○ Audiobook

Title... _____

Author... _____

○ Fiction: ○ Non-Fiction:
   Genre. . . . .   Subject. . . . .

5	5	5	5	5	5	5	5	5	5	5	5	5	5	5	5	5	5	5	5	5	5	5	5	Total
5	5	5	5	5	5	5	5	5	5	5	5	5	5	5	5	5	5	5	5	5	5	5	5	

71

Color the stars to rate this book
1 Star = Hated it   5 Stars = Loved it

Date Started . . . .

Date Finished . . . .

How I Got This Book:

○ Bought it

○ Checked out from library

○ Borrowed from

. . . .

○ Gift from:

. . . .

What I Liked About This Book...

. . . .
. . . .
. . . .
. . . .
. . . .
. . . .

This Book Was Easy To Read
○ Yes   ○ No

I Was Really Surprised When...

. . . .
. . . .
. . . .
. . . .

Stuff I Learned From This Book:

. . . .
. . . .

My Favorite Character Was...

. . . .

I Liked Them Because...

. . . .
. . . .
. . . .

Favorite Quote From The Book:

. . . .

It Was Funny/Sad/Happy When They...

. . . .
. . . .
. . . .
. . . .

○ Paperback ○ Hardback ○ Ebook ○ Audiobook

Color the stars to rate this book
1 Star = Hated it   5 Stars = Loved it

Title..._____

Author..._____

○ Fiction:
   Genre...............

○ Non-Fiction:
   Subject...............

Date Started...............

Date Finished...............

5	5	5	5	5	5	5	5	5	5	5	5	5	5	5	5	5	5	5	5	5	5	5	5	Total
5	5	5	5	5	5	5	5	5	5	5	5	5	5	5	5	5	5	5	5	5	5	5	5	

←————//————→

How I Got This Book:

○ Bought it

○ Checked out from library

○ Borrowed from

....

○ Gift from:

....

←————//————→

This Book Was Easy To Read
○ Yes   ○ No

←————//————→

Stuff I Learned From This Book:

....
....
....
....
....

Favorite Quote From The Book:

....
....
....

What I Liked About This Book...

....
....
....
....
....

I Was Really Surprised When...

....
....

My Favorite Character Was...

I Liked Them Because...

....

It Was Funny/Sad/Happy When They...

....
....
....
....

○ Paperback ○ Hardback ○ Ebook ○ Audiobook

Title.._____

Author.._____

○ Fiction: ○ Non-Fiction:
   Genre. . . . .   Subject. . . . .

| 5 | 5 | 5 | 5 | 5 | 5 | 5 | 5 | 5 | 5 | 5 | 5 | 5 | 5 | 5 | 5 | 5 | 5 | 5 | 5 | 5 | 5 | 5 | 5 | 5 | Total |
| 5 | 5 | 5 | 5 | 5 | 5 | 5 | 5 | 5 | 5 | 5 | 5 | 5 | 5 | 5 | 5 | 5 | 5 | 5 | 5 | 5 | 5 | 5 | 5 | 5 | |

73

Color the stars to rate this book
1 Star = Hated it   5 Stars = Loved it

What I Liked About This Book...

. . . .
. . . .
. . . .
. . . .
. . . .
. . . .
. . . .

I Was Really Surprised When...

. . . .
. . . .
. . . .

My Favorite Character Was...

. . . .

I Liked Them Because...

. . . .
. . . .
. . . .

It Was Funny/Sad/Happy When They...

. . . .
. . . .
. . . .
. . . .

Date Started . . . .
Date Finished. . . . .
←———————//———————→
How I Got This Book:
○ Bought it
○ Checked out from library
○ Borrowed from

. . . .
○ Gift from:

. . . .
←———————//———————→
This Book Was Easy To Read
○ Yes   ○ No
←———————//———————→
Stuff I Learned From This Book:

. . . .
. . . .
. . . .
. . . .

Favorite Quote From The Book:

. . . .
. . . .
. . . .
. . . .

○ Paperback   ○ Hardback   ○ Ebook   ○ Audiobook

74

Color the stars to rate this book
1 Star = Hated it   5 Stars = Loved it

Title..._____ ✎

Author..._____ ✎

○ Fiction: ○ Non-Fiction:
   Genre. . . . .   Subject. . . . .

Date Started . . . .

Date Finished . . . .

S	S	S	S	S	S	S	S	S	S	S	S	S	S	S	S	S	S	S	S	S	S	S	S	Total
S	S	S	S	S	S	S	S	S	S	S	S	S	S	S	S	S	S	S	S	S	S	S	S	

←————— // —————→

How I Got This Book:

○ Bought it

○ Checked out from library

○ Borrowed from

. . . .

○ Gift from:

←————— // —————→

This Book Was Easy To Read
○ Yes   ○ No

←————— // —————→

Stuff I Learned From This Book:

. . . .
. . . .
. . . .
. . . .
. . . .

Favorite Quote From The Book:

. . . .
. . . .

What I Liked About This Book...

. . . .
. . . .
. . . .
. . . .
. . . .
. . . .

I Was Really Surprised When...

. . . .
. . . .
. . . .

My Favorite Character Was...

I Liked Them Because...

. . . .

It Was Funny/Sad/Happy When They...

. . . .
. . . .
. . . .

○ Paperback ○ Hardback ○ Ebook ○ Audiobook

Title..._____

Author..._____

○ Fiction: ○ Non-Fiction:
  Genre. . . . .   Subject. . . . .

5	5	5	5	5	5	5	5	5	5	5	5	5	5	5	5	5	5	5	5	5	5	5	5	5	Total
5	5	5	5	5	5	5	5	5	5	5	5	5	5	5	5	5	5	5	5	5	5	5	5	5	

75

Color the stars to rate this book
1 Star = Hated it   5 Stars = Loved it

What I Liked About This Book...

. . . .
. . . .
. . . .
. . . .
. . . .
. . . .

Date Started . . . .

Date Finished . . . .

How I Got This Book:

○ Bought it

○ Checked out from library

○ Borrowed from

. . . .

○ Gift from:

. . . .

I Was Really Surprised When...

. . . .
. . . .
. . . .

This Book Was Easy To Read
○ Yes   ○ No

Stuff I Learned From This Book:

. . . .

. . . .

My Favorite Character Was...

. . . .

. . . .

I Liked Them Because...

. . . .
. . . .

Favorite Quote From The Book:

It Was Funny/Sad/Happy When They...

. . . .
. . . .
. . . .
. . . .

○ Paperback ○ Hardback ○ Ebook ○ Audiobook

76

Color the stars to rate this book
1 Star = Hated it   5 Stars = Loved it

Date Started . . . .

Date Finished . . . .

⟵——————//——————⟶

How I Got This Book:

○ Bought it

○ Checked out from library

○ Borrowed from

. . . .

○ Gift from:

. . . .

⟵——————//——————⟶

This Book Was Easy To Read
○ Yes   ○ No

⟵——————//——————⟶

Stuff I Learned From This Book:

. . . .

. . . .

. . . .

. . . .

. . . .

. . . .

Favorite Quote From The Book:

. . . .

. . . .

. . . .

. . . .

. . . .

Title . . . _____

Author . . . _____

○ Fiction: ○ Non-Fiction:
   Genre . . . .   Subject . . . .

5	5	5	5	5	5	5	5	5	5	5	5	5	5	5	5	5	5	5	5	5	5	5	Total
5	5	5	5	5	5	5	5	5	5	5	5	5	5	5	5	5	5	5	5	5	5	5	

What I Liked About This Book...

. . . .

. . . .

. . . .

. . . .

. . . .

. . . .

. . . .

I Was Really Surprised When...

. . . .

. . . .

. . . .

My Favorite Character Was...

I Liked Them Because...

. . . .

. . . .

It Was Funny/Sad/Happy When They...

. . . .

. . . .

. . . .

○ Paperback ○ Hardback ○ Ebook ○ Audiobook

Title... _____

Author... _____

○ Fiction:
    Genre....................

○ Non-Fiction:
    Subject..................

5	5	5	5	5	5	5	5	5	5	5	5	5	5	5	5	5	5	5	5	5	5	5	5	5	Total
5	5	5	5	5	5	5	5	5	5	5	5	5	5	5	5	5	5	5	5	5	5	5	5	5	

77

Color the stars to rate this book
1 Star = Hated it   5 Stars = Loved it

Date Started ....

Date Finished...............

How I Got This Book:
○ Bought it
○ Checked out from library
○ Borrowed from
....
○ Gift from:
....

This Book Was Easy To Read
○ Yes   ○ No

What I Liked About This Book...

....
....
....
....
....
....

I Was Really Surprised When...

....
....
....

Stuff I Learned From This Book:
....
....
....

My Favorite Character Was...

....

I Liked Them Because...

....
....

Favorite Quote From The Book:

It Was Funny/Sad/Happy When They...

....
....
....
....
....

○ Paperback ○ Hardback ○ Ebook ○ Audiobook

78

Color the stars to rate this book
1 Star = Hated it   5 Stars = Loved it

Date Started . . . .

Date Finished . . . .

⟵————//————⟶

How I Got This Book:

○ Bought it

○ Checked out from library

○ Borrowed from

. . . .

○ Gift from:

. . . .

⟵————//————⟶

This Book Was Easy To Read
○ Yes   ○ No

⟵————//————⟶

Stuff I Learned From This Book:

. . . .

. . . .

. . . .

. . . .

. . . .

. . . .

Favorite Quote From The Book:

. . . .

. . . .

. . . .

. . . .

Title . . . _____

Author . . . _____

○ Fiction: ○ Non-Fiction:
   Genre . . . .   Subject . . . .

S	S	S	S	S	S	S	S	S	S	S	S	S	S	S	S	S	S	S	S	S	S	S	S	S	Total
S	S	S	S	S	S	S	S	S	S	S	S	S	S	S	S	S	S	S	S	S	S	S	S	S	

What I Liked About This Book...

. . . .

. . . .

. . . .

. . . .

. . . .

. . . .

. . . .

I Was Really Surprised When...

. . . .

. . . .

My Favorite Character Was...

I Liked Them Because...

. . . .

. . . .

It Was Funny/Sad/Happy When They...

. . . .

. . . .

. . . .

○ Paperback   ○ Hardback   ○ Ebook   ○ Audiobook

Title..._____

Author..._____

○ Fiction: ○ Non-Fiction:
   Genre................   Subject................

79

Color the stars to rate this book
1 Star = Hated it   5 Stars = Loved it

5	5	5	5	5	5	5	5	5	5	5	5	5	5	5	5	5	5	5	5	5	5	5	5	Total
5	5	5	5	5	5	5	5	5	5	5	5	5	5	5	5	5	5	5	5	5	5	5	5	

Date Started................

Date Finished...............

What I Liked About This Book...

....
....
....
....
....
....
....

How I Got This Book:

○ Bought it

○ Checked out from library

○ Borrowed from

....

○ Gift from:

....

I Was Really Surprised When...

....
....
....

This Book Was Easy To Read
○ Yes   ○ No

Stuff I Learned From This Book:

....

My Favorite Character Was...

....

I Liked Them Because...

....
....
....

Favorite Quote From The Book:

....

It Was Funny/Sad/Happy When They...

....
....
....
....

....

80

Color the stars to rate this book
1 Star = Hated it   5 Stars = Loved it

Date Started . . . .

Date Finished . . . .

⟵————— // —————⟶

How I Got This Book:

○ Bought it

○ Checked out from library

○ Borrowed from

. . . .

○ Gift from:

. . . .

⟵————— // —————⟶

This Book Was Easy To Read

○ Yes   ○ No

⟵————— // —————⟶

Stuff I Learned From This Book:

. . . .

. . . .

. . . .

. . . .

. . . .

. . . .

Favorite Quote From The Book:

. . . .

. . . .

. . . .

. . . .

. . . .

Title... _____ ✎

Author... _____ ✎

○ Fiction: ○ Non-Fiction:

Genre. . . . .   Subject. . . . .

5	5	5	5	5	5	5	5	5	5	5	5	5	5	5	5	5	5	5	5	5	5	5	5	Total
5	5	5	5	5	5	5	5	5	5	5	5	5	5	5	5	5	5	5	5	5	5	5	5	

What I Liked About This Book...

. . . .

. . . .

. . . .

. . . .

. . . .

. . . .

I Was Really Surprised When...

. . . .

. . . .

. . . .

My Favorite Character Was...

I Liked Them Because...

. . . .

It Was Funny/Sad/Happy When They...

. . . .

. . . .

. . . .

◯ Paperback ◯ Hardback ◯ Ebook ◯ Audiobook

Title..._____

Author.._____

◯ Fiction: ◯ Non-Fiction:
  Genre.................   Subject................

5	5	5	5	5	5	5	5	5	5	5	5	5	5	5	5	5	5	5	5	5	5	5	5	5	Total
5	5	5	5	5	5	5	5	5	5	5	5	5	5	5	5	5	5	5	5	5	5	5	5	5	

81

Color the stars to rate this book
1 Star = Hated it   5 Stars = Loved it

What I Liked About This Book...

....
....
....
....
....
....
....

I Was Really Surprised When...

....
....
....
....

My Favorite Character Was...

....

I Liked Them Because...

....
....
....

It Was Funny/Sad/Happy When They...

....
....
....
....

Date Started ....
Date Finished...............
←————//————→
How I Got This Book:
◯ Bought it
◯ Checked out from library
◯ Borrowed from

....
◯ Gift from:

....
←————//————→
This Book Was Easy To Read
◯ Yes   ◯ No
←————//————→
Stuff I Learned From This Book:
....
....
....
....
....
....
....

Favorite Quote From The Book:
....
....
....
....

○ Paperback ○ Hardback ○ Ebook ○ Audiobook

Color the stars to rate this book
1 Star = Hated it   5 Stars = Loved it

Date Started . . . .

Date Finished . . . .

←——————//——————→

How I Got This Book:

○ Bought it

○ Checked out from library

○ Borrowed from

. . . .

○ Gift from:

. . . .

←——————//——————→

This Book Was Easy To Read
○ Yes   ○ No

←——————//——————→

Stuff I Learned From This Book:

. . . .

. . . .

. . . .

. . . .

. . . .

. . . .

. . . .

. . . .

Favorite Quote From The Book:

. . . .

. . . .

. . . .

. . . .

. . . .

Title . . . _____

Author . . . _____

○ Fiction: ○ Non-Fiction:
   Genre . . . .   Subject . . . .

																								Total
5	5	5	5	5	5	5	5	5	5	5	5	5	5	5	5	5	5	5	5	5	5	5	5	5	
5	5	5	5	5	5	5	5	5	5	5	5	5	5	5	5	5	5	5	5	5	5	5	5	5	

What I Liked About This Book...

. . . .

. . . .

. . . .

. . . .

. . . .

I Was Really Surprised When...

. . . .

My Favorite Character Was...

I Liked Them Because...

. . . .

It Was Funny/Sad/Happy When They...

. . . .

. . . .

. . . .

○ Paperback ○ Hardback ○ Ebook ○ Audiobook

Title...

Author...

○ Fiction:
Genre.................

○ Non-Fiction:
Subject................

Color the stars to rate this book
1 Star = Hated it   5 Stars = Loved it

83

5	5	5	5	5	5	5	5	5	5	5	5	5	5	5	5	5	5	5	5	5	5	5	5	Total
5	5	5	5	5	5	5	5	5	5	5	5	5	5	5	5	5	5	5	5	5	5	5	5	

Date Started................

Date Finished...............

←——————//——————→

How I Got This Book:

○ Bought it

○ Checked out from library

○ Borrowed from

....

○ Gift from:

....

←——————//——————→

This Book Was Easy To Read

○ Yes   ○ No

←——————//——————→

What I Liked About This Book...

....
....
....
....
....
....
....
....

I Was Really Surprised When...

....
....
....
....

Stuff I Learned From This Book:

....
....
....

My Favorite Character Was...

....

I Liked Them Because...

....
....

Favorite Quote From The Book:

....

It Was Funny/Sad/Happy When They...

....
....
....
....

○ Paperback ○ Hardback ○ Ebook ○ Audiobook

84

Color the stars to rate this book
1 Star = Hated it   5 Stars = Loved it

Title..._____

Author..._____

○ Fiction:
   Genre. . . . .

○ Non-Fiction:
   Subject. . . . .

| 5 | 5 | 5 | 5 | 5 | 5 | 5 | 5 | 5 | 5 | 5 | 5 | 5 | 5 | 5 | 5 | 5 | 5 | 5 | 5 | 5 | 5 | 5 | 5 | Total |
| 5 | 5 | 5 | 5 | 5 | 5 | 5 | 5 | 5 | 5 | 5 | 5 | 5 | 5 | 5 | 5 | 5 | 5 | 5 | 5 | 5 | 5 | 5 | 5 | |

Date Started . . . .

Date Finished. . . . .

⟵————————//————————⟶

How I Got This Book:

○ Bought it

○ Checked out from library

○ Borrowed from
. . . .

○ Gift from:
. . . .

⟵————————//————————⟶

This Book Was Easy To Read
○ Yes   ○ No
⟵————————//————————⟶

Stuff I Learned From This Book:
. . . .
. . . .
. . . .
. . . .
. . . .
. . . .

Favorite Quote From The Book:
. . . .
. . . .
. . . .
. . . .

What I Liked About This Book...
. . . .
. . . .
. . . .
. . . .
. . . .
. . . .

I Was Really Surprised When...
. . . .
. . . .
. . . .

My Favorite Character Was...

I Liked Them Because...
. . . .
. . . .

It Was Funny/Sad/Happy When They...
. . . .
. . . .
. . . .

○ Paperback ○ Hardback ○ Ebook ○ Audiobook

Title..._____

Author..._____

○ Fiction:
Genre................

○ Non-Fiction:
Subject................

| 5 | 5 | 5 | 5 | 5 | 5 | 5 | 5 | 5 | 5 | 5 | 5 | 5 | 5 | 5 | 5 | 5 | 5 | 5 | 5 | 5 | 5 | 5 | 5 | 5 | 5 | 5 | Total |
| 5 | 5 | 5 | 5 | 5 | 5 | 5 | 5 | 5 | 5 | 5 | 5 | 5 | 5 | 5 | 5 | 5 | 5 | 5 | 5 | 5 | 5 | 5 | 5 | 5 | 5 | 5 | |

85

Color the stars to rate this book
1 Star = Hated it 5 Stars = Loved it

What I Liked About This Book...

....
....
....
....
....
....
....
....
....

I Was Really Surprised When...

....
....
....

My Favorite Character Was...

....

I Liked Them Because...

....
....
....

It Was Funny/Sad/Happy When They...

....
....
....

Date Started ....
Date Finished ....

←————//————→

How I Got This Book:

○ Bought it

○ Checked out from library

○ Borrowed from

....

○ Gift from:

....

←————//————→

This Book Was Easy To Read
○ Yes   ○ No

←————//————→

Stuff I Learned From This Book:

....
....
....
....
....

Favorite Quote From The Book:

....
....
....
....

○ Paperback ○ Hardback ○ Ebook ○ Audiobook

Color the stars to rate this book
1 Star = Hated it   5 Stars = Loved it

Date Started . . . .

Date Finished . . . .

How I Got This Book:
○ Bought it
○ Checked out from library
○ Borrowed from
. . . .
○ Gift from:
. . . .

This Book Was Easy To Read
○ Yes   ○ No

Stuff I Learned From This Book:
. . . .
. . . .
. . . .
. . . .
. . . .
. . . .

Favorite Quote From The Book:
. . . .
. . . .
. . . .
. . . .
. . . .

Title... _____

Author... _____

○ Fiction: ○ Non-Fiction:
  Genre. . . . .   Subject. . . . .

S	S	S	S	S	S	S	S	S	S	S	S	S	S	S	S	S	S	S	S	S	S	S	Total
S	S	S	S	S	S	S	S	S	S	S	S	S	S	S	S	S	S	S	S	S	S	S	

What I Liked About This Book...
. . . .
. . . .
. . . .
. . . .
. . . .
. . . .

I Was Really Surprised When...
. . . .
. . . .
. . . .

My Favorite Character Was...

I Liked Them Because...
. . . .

It Was Funny/Sad/Happy When They...
. . . .
. . . .
. . . .

○ Paperback ○ Hardback ○ Ebook ○ Audiobook

Title..._____

Author.._____

○ Fiction:
  Genre.................

○ Non-Fiction:
  Subject................

5	5	5	5	5	5	5	5	5	5	5	5	5	5	5	5	5	5	5	5	5	5	5	5	5	5	Total
5	5	5	5	5	5	5	5	5	5	5	5	5	5	5	5	5	5	5	5	5	5	5	5	5	5	

87

Color the stars to rate this book
1 Star = Hated it   5 Stars = Loved it

What I Liked About This Book...

....
....
....
....
....
....
....
....

I Was Really Surprised When...

....
....
....

My Favorite Character Was...

....

I Liked Them Because...

....
....

It Was Funny/Sad/Happy When They...

....
....
....
....

Date Started ....

Date Finished...............

How I Got This Book:

○ Bought it

○ Checked out from library

○ Borrowed from

....

○ Gift from:

....

This Book Was Easy To Read
○ Yes   ○ No

Stuff I Learned From This Book:

....
....
....
....
....

Favorite Quote From The Book:

....
....

○ Paperback ○ Hardback ○ Ebook ○ Audiobook

88

Color the stars to rate this book
1 Star = Hated it   5 Stars = Loved it

Date Started . . . .

Date Finished . . . .

How I Got This Book:

○ Bought it

○ Checked out from library

○ Borrowed from

. . . .

○ Gift from:

. . . .

This Book Was Easy To Read
○ Yes   ○ No

Stuff I Learned From This Book:

. . . .
. . . .
. . . .
. . . .
. . . .
. . . .
. . . .

Favorite Quote From The Book:

. . . .
. . . .
. . . .
. . . .
. . . .

Title.. _____

Author.. _____

○ Fiction: ○ Non-Fiction:
  Genre. . . . .   Subject. . . . .

5	5	5	5	5	5	5	5	5	5	5	5	5	5	5	5	5	5	5	5	5	5	5	Total
5	5	5	5	5	5	5	5	5	5	5	5	5	5	5	5	5	5	5	5	5	5	5	

What I Liked About This Book...

. . . .
. . . .
. . . .
. . . .
. . . .
. . . .

I Was Really Surprised When...

. . . .
. . . .
. . . .

My Favorite Character Was...

I Liked Them Because...

. . . .
. . . .

It Was Funny/Sad/Happy When They...

. . . .
. . . .
. . . .
. . . .

○ Paperback ○ Hardback ○ Ebook ○ Audiobook

Title..._____

Author.._____

○ Fiction: ○ Non-Fiction:
   Genre. . . . .   Subject. . . . .

5	5	5	5	5	5	5	5	5	5	5	5	5	5	5	5	5	5	5	5	5	5	5	5	Total
5	5	5	5	5	5	5	5	5	5	5	5	5	5	5	5	5	5	5	5	5	5	5	5	

89

Color the stars to rate this book
1 Star = Hated it   5 Stars = Loved it

What I Liked About This Book...

. . . .
. . . .
. . . .
. . . .
. . . .
. . . .
. . . .

Date Started . . . .
Date Finished. . . . .
←——————//——————→
How I Got This Book:
○ Bought it
○ Checked out from library
○ Borrowed from
. . . .
○ Gift from:
. . . .
←——————//——————→
This Book Was Easy To Read
○ Yes   ○ No
←——————//——————→
Stuff I Learned From This Book:

I Was Really Surprised When...

. . . .
. . . .
. . . .

. . . .
. . . .

My Favorite Character Was...

. . . .

I Liked Them Because...

. . . .
. . . .

. . . .

Favorite Quote From The Book:

It Was Funny/Sad/Happy When They...

. . . .
. . . .
. . . .
. . . .

. . . .

Color the stars to rate this book
1 Star = Hated it   5 Stars = Loved it

Date Started . . . .

Date Finished . . . .

←——————//——————→

How I Got This Book:

◯ Bought it

◯ Checked out from library

◯ Borrowed from

. . . .

◯ Gift from:

. . . .

←——————//——————→

This Book Was Easy To Read
◯ Yes   ◯ No

←——————//——————→

Stuff I Learned From This Book:

. . . .

. . . .

. . . .

. . . .

. . . .

. . . .

Favorite Quote From The Book:

. . . .

. . . .

. . . .

. . . .

. . . .

◯ Paperback   ◯ Hardback   ◯ Ebook   ◯ Audiobook

Title... _____

Author... _____

◯ Fiction: ◯ Non-Fiction:
   Genre . . . .   Subject . . . .

5	5	5	5	5	5	5	5	5	5	5	5	5	5	5	5	5	5	5	5	5	5	5	5	Total
5	5	5	5	5	5	5	5	5	5	5	5	5	5	5	5	5	5	5	5	5	5	5	5	

What I Liked About This Book...

. . . .

. . . .

. . . .

. . . .

. . . .

. . . .

I Was Really Surprised When...

. . . .

. . . .

My Favorite Character Was...

I Liked Them Because...

. . . .

. . . .

It Was Funny/Sad/Happy When They...

. . . .

. . . .

. . . .

. . . .

◌ Paperback ◌ Hardback ◌ Ebook ◌ Audiobook

Title... _____

Author.._____

◌ Fiction: ◌ Non-Fiction:
  Genre.................   Subject.................

| 5 | 5 | 5 | 5 | 5 | 5 | 5 | 5 | 5 | 5 | 5 | 5 | 5 | 5 | 5 | 5 | 5 | 5 | 5 | 5 | 5 | 5 | 5 | 5 | 5 | Total |
| 5 | 5 | 5 | 5 | 5 | 5 | 5 | 5 | 5 | 5 | 5 | 5 | 5 | 5 | 5 | 5 | 5 | 5 | 5 | 5 | 5 | 5 | 5 | 5 | 5 | |

91

Color the stars to rate this book
1 Star = Hated it   5 Stars = Loved it

Date Started ....

Date Finished...............
←——————//——————→
How I Got This Book:
◌ Bought it
◌ Checked out from library
◌ Borrowed from
  ....
◌ Gift from:
  ....
←——————//——————→
This Book Was Easy To Read
◌ Yes   ◌ No
←——————//——————→
Stuff I Learned From This Book:

What I Liked About This Book...

....
....
....
....
....
....

....
....
....
....

I Was Really Surprised When...

....
....
....
....

My Favorite Character Was...

I Liked Them Because...

....
....

Favorite Quote From The Book:
....

It Was Funny/Sad/Happy When They...

....
....
....
....

○ Paperback   ○ Hardback   ○ Ebook   ○ Audiobook

Color the stars to rate this book
1 Star = Hated it   5 Stars = Loved it

Title..._____ ✏

Author..._____ ✏

○ Fiction: ○ Non-Fiction:
   Genre. . . . .   Subject. . . . .

Date Started . . . .

Date Finished. . . . .

S	S	S	S	S	S	S	S	S	S	S	S	S	S	S	S	S	S	S	S	S	S	S	S	Total
S	S	S	S	S	S	S	S	S	S	S	S	S	S	S	S	S	S	S	S	S	S	S	S	

←——————//——————→

How I Got This Book:
○ Bought it
○ Checked out from library
○ Borrowed from
   . . . .
○ Gift from:
   . . . .

←——————//——————→

This Book Was Easy To Read
○ Yes   ○ No

←——————//——————→

Stuff I Learned From This Book:
. . . .
. . . .
. . . .
. . . .
. . . .
. . . .

Favorite Quote From The Book:
. . . .
. . . .
. . . .
. . . .
. . . .

What I Liked About This Book...

. . . .
. . . .
. . . .
. . . .
. . . .
. . . .
. . . .

I Was Really Surprised When...

. . . .
. . . .
. . . .

My Favorite Character Was...

I Liked Them Because...

. . . .
. . . .

It Was Funny/Sad/Happy When They...

. . . .
. . . .
. . . .

◯ Paperback ◯ Hardback ◯ Ebook ◯ Audiobook

Title..._____

Author.._____

◯ Fiction: ◯ Non-Fiction:
  Genre. . . . .   Subject. . . . .

93

Color the stars to rate this book
1 Star = Hated it   5 Stars = Loved it

5	5	5	5	5	5	5	5	5	5	5	5	5	5	5	5	5	5	5	5	5	5	5	5	5	Total
5	5	5	5	5	5	5	5	5	5	5	5	5	5	5	5	5	5	5	5	5	5	5	5	5	

What I Liked About This Book...

. . . .
. . . .
. . . .
. . . .
. . . .
. . . .
. . . .

Date Started . . . .
Date Finished. . . . .
←————————//————————→
How I Got This Book:
◯ Bought it
◯ Checked out from library
◯ Borrowed from
. . . .
◯ Gift from:
. . . .
←————————//————————→

I Was Really Surprised When...

. . . .
. . . .
. . . .
. . . .

This Book Was Easy To Read
◯ Yes   ◯ No
←————————//————————→
Stuff I Learned From This Book:
. . . .
. . . .
. . . .

My Favorite Character Was...

. . . .

. . . .

I Liked Them Because...

. . . .
. . . .

. . . .

Favorite Quote From The Book:

It Was Funny/Sad/Happy When They...

. . . .

. . . .
. . . .
. . . .
. . . .

○ Paperback   ○ Hardback   ○ Ebook   ○ Audiobook

94

Color the stars to rate this book
1 Star = Hated it   5 Stars = Loved it

Title... _____

Author... _____

○ Fiction: ○ Non-Fiction:
   Genre. . . . .   Subject. . . . .

Date Started . . . .

Date Finished. . . . .

5	5	5	5	5	5	5	5	5	5	5	5	5	5	5	5	5	5	5	5	5	5	5	5	Total
5	5	5	5	5	5	5	5	5	5	5	5	5	5	5	5	5	5	5	5	5	5	5	5	

How I Got This Book:

○ Bought it

○ Checked out from library

○ Borrowed from

. . . .

○ Gift from:

. . . .

This Book Was Easy To Read
○ Yes   ○ No

Stuff I Learned From This Book:

. . . .

. . . .

. . . .

. . . .

. . . .

. . . .

Favorite Quote From The Book:

. . . .

. . . .

. . . .

. . . .

What I Liked About This Book...

. . . .

. . . .

. . . .

. . . .

. . . .

. . . .

. . . .

I Was Really Surprised When...

. . . .

. . . .

. . . .

My Favorite Character Was...

I Liked Them Because...

. . . .

. . . .

It Was Funny/Sad/Happy When They...

. . . .

. . . .

. . . .

○ Paperback ○ Hardback ○ Ebook ○ Audiobook

Title..._____

Author.._____

○ Fiction: ○ Non-Fiction:
  Genre.................   Subject.................

5	5	5	5	5	5	5	5	5	5	5	5	5	5	5	5	5	5	5	5	5	5	5	5	5	Total
5	5	5	5	5	5	5	5	5	5	5	5	5	5	5	5	5	5	5	5	5	5	5	5	5	

What I Liked About This Book...

. . . .
. . . .
. . . .
. . . .
. . . .
. . . .
. . . .

I Was Really Surprised When...

. . . .
. . . .
. . . .

My Favorite Character Was...

. . . .

I Liked Them Because...

. . . .
. . . .

It Was Funny/Sad/Happy When They...

. . . .
. . . .
. . . .
. . . .

95

Color the stars to rate this book
1 Star = Hated it   5 Stars = Loved it

Date Started . . . .

Date Finished . . . .

←——————//——————→

How I Got This Book:

○ Bought it

○ Checked out from library

○ Borrowed from

. . . .

○ Gift from:

. . . .

←——————//——————→

This Book Was Easy To Read

○ Yes   ○ No

←——————//——————→

Stuff I Learned From This Book:

. . . .
. . . .
. . . .
. . . .

Favorite Quote From The Book:

. . . .
. . . .

Color the stars to rate this book
1 Star = Hated it   5 Stars = Loved it

Date Started . . . .

Date Finished . . . .

←——————//——————→

How I Got This Book:
◯ Bought it
◯ Checked out from library
◯ Borrowed from
. . . .
◯ Gift from:
. . . .

←——————//——————→

This Book Was Easy To Read
◯ Yes   ◯ No

←——————//——————→

Stuff I Learned From This Book:
. . . .
. . . .
. . . .
. . . .
. . . .

Favorite Quote From The Book:
. . . .
. . . .
. . . .
. . . .

◯ Paperback ◯ Hardback ◯ Ebook ◯ Audiobook

Title . . . _____

Author . . . _____

◯ Fiction: ◯ Non-Fiction:
   Genre . . . .   Subject . . . .

5	5	5	5	5	5	5	5	5	5	5	5	5	5	5	5	5	5	5	5	5	5	5	5	5	Total
5	5	5	5	5	5	5	5	5	5	5	5	5	5	5	5	5	5	5	5	5	5	5	5	5	

What I Liked About This Book...
. . . .
. . . .
. . . .
. . . .
. . . .
. . . .
. . . .

I Was Really Surprised When...
. . . .
. . . .
. . . .

My Favorite Character Was...
. . . .

I Liked Them Because...
. . . .
. . . .

It Was Funny/Sad/Happy When They...
. . . .
. . . .
. . . .

○ Paperback ○ Hardback ○ Ebook ○ Audiobook

Title... _____

Author... _____

○ Fiction: ○ Non-Fiction:
  Genre. . . . .   Subject. . . . .

5	5	5	5	5	5	5	5	5	5	5	5	5	5	5	5	5	5	5	5	5	5	5	5	5	Total
5	5	5	5	5	5	5	5	5	5	5	5	5	5	5	5	5	5	5	5	5	5	5	5	5	

97

Color the stars to rate this book
1 Star = Hated it   5 Stars = Loved it

Date Started . . . .
Date Finished . . . .
←————— // —————→
How I Got This Book:
○ Bought it
○ Checked out from library
○ Borrowed from
. . . .
○ Gift from:
. . . .
←————— // —————→
This Book Was Easy To Read
○ Yes   ○ No
←————— // —————→
Stuff I Learned From This Book:

What I Liked About This Book...

. . . .
. . . .
. . . .
. . . .
. . . .
. . . .
. . . .

I Was Really Surprised When...

. . . .
. . . .
. . . .
. . . .

My Favorite Character Was...

. . . .

I Liked Them Because...

. . . .
. . . .

Favorite Quote From The Book:

It Was Funny/Sad/Happy When They...

. . . .
. . . .
. . . .
. . . .

○ Paperback ○ Hardback ○ Ebook ○ Audiobook

98

Color the stars to rate this book
I Star = Hated it   5 Stars = Loved it

Date Started . . . .

Date Finished . . . .

How I Got This Book:
○ Bought it
○ Checked out from library
○ Borrowed from
. . . .
○ Gift from:
. . . .

This Book Was Easy To Read
○ Yes   ○ No

Stuff I Learned From This Book:
. . . .
. . . .
. . . .
. . . .
. . . .
. . . .

Favorite Quote From The Book:
. . . .
. . . .
. . . .
. . . .

Title . . . _____

Author . . . _____

○ Fiction: ○ Non-Fiction:
   Genre . . . .   Subject . . . .

5	5	5	5	5	5	5	5	5	5	5	5	5	5	5	5	5	5	5	5	5	5	5	Total
5	5	5	5	5	5	5	5	5	5	5	5	5	5	5	5	5	5	5	5	5	5	5	

What I Liked About This Book...

. . . .
. . . .
. . . .
. . . .
. . . .
. . . .

I Was Really Surprised When...

. . . .
. . . .
. . . .

My Favorite Character Was...

I Liked Them Because...

. . . .

It Was Funny/Sad/Happy When They...

. . . .
. . . .
. . . .
. . . .

○ Paperback ○ Hardback ○ Ebook ○ Audiobook

Title..._____

Author..._____

○ Fiction: ○ Non-Fiction:
    Genre.................   Subject................

5	5	5	5	5	5	5	5	5	5	5	5	5	5	5	5	5	5	5	5	5	5	5	Total
5	5	5	5	5	5	5	5	5	5	5	5	5	5	5	5	5	5	5	5	5	5	5	

What I Liked About This Book...

....
....
....
....
....
....
....
....

I Was Really Surprised When...

....
....
....
....

My Favorite Character Was...

....

I Liked Them Because...

....
....
....

It Was Funny/Sad/Happy When They...

....
....
....
....

99

Color the stars to rate this book
1 Star = Hated it   5 Stars = Loved it

Date Started ....

Date Finished................

←————//————→

How I Got This Book:

○ Bought it

○ Checked out from library

○ Borrowed from

....

○ Gift from:

....

←————//————→

This Book Was Easy To Read
○ Yes   ○ No

←————//————→

Stuff I Learned From This Book:

....
....
....
....
....

Favorite Quote From The Book:

....
....

100

Color the stars to rate this book
1 Star = Hated it   5 Stars = Loved it

Date Started . . . .

Date Finished . . . .

How I Got This Book:

◯ Bought it

◯ Checked out from library

◯ Borrowed from

. . . .

◯ Gift from:

. . . .

This Book Was Easy To Read

◯ Yes   ◯ No

Stuff I Learned From This Book:

. . . .
. . . .
. . . .
. . . .
. . . .
. . . .
. . . .

Favorite Quote From The Book:

. . . .
. . . .
. . . .
. . . .

◯ Paperback ◯ Hardback ◯ Ebook ◯ Audiobook

Title . . . _____ ✎

Author . . . _____ ✎

◯ Fiction: ◯ Non-Fiction:
   Genre . . . .   Subject . . . .

5	5	5	5	5	5	5	5	5	5	5	5	5	5	5	5	5	5	5	5	5	5	5	5	Total
5	5	5	5	5	5	5	5	5	5	5	5	5	5	5	5	5	5	5	5	5	5	5	5	

What I Liked About This Book...

. . . .
. . . .
. . . .
. . . .
. . . .
. . . .
. . . .

I Was Really Surprised When...

. . . .
. . . .
. . . .

My Favorite Character Was...

I Liked Them Because...

. . . .

It Was Funny/Sad/Happy When They...

. . . .
. . . .
. . . .

BOOK LOAN SHEET

BOOK NUMBER	BOOK TITLE	LOANED TO	DATE

Dear Book Lover,

We hope you have enjoyed using your reading log and that you had a good time reading lots of books.

We are a small husband and wife business. Words cannot express how much we appreciate that you used our book to track your reading.

It would help us a lot if you could ask the person who bought this book for you to take a moment and leave a review about this book on Amazon.

Thanks again, Belle Journals
@bellejournals

READING LOG FOR KIDS • BOOK 7

CONNECT WITH US

BELLEJOURNALS.COM/BOOKS
FACEBOOK.COM/BELLEJOURNALS
INSTAGRAM.COM/BELLEJOURNALS
PINTEREST.COM/BELLEJOURNALS
TWITTER.COM/BELLEJOURNALS

SCAN THE CODE BELOW TO SEE MORE
READING LOGS FOR KIDS

· ·

OUR COLLECTION OF BOOKS INCLUDE:
5MM DOT GRID JOURNALS, COLLEGE RULED LINED NOTEBOOKS,
ONE LINE A DAY/WEEK JOURNALS, BLANK STORY BOOKS,
DAY PLANNERS, GUEST BOOKS, PRAYER JOURNALS,
SERMON NOTES, MILEAGE LOGS, SPORTS MEMORY BOOKS
AND MANY MORE.

SOME OF OUR BOOKS ARE AVAILABLE
IN OTHER SIZES AND STYLES

YOUR SUGGESTIONS ARE WELCOME – WRITE US AT:
BOOKS@BELLEJOURNALS.COM

Made in the USA
Monee, IL
21 December 2022

23153328R00063